ART IDEAS HISTORY

THE MAKING OF
THE CHRISTIAN WEST

980-1140

GEORGES DUBY

TRANSLATED FROM THE FRENCH BY STUART GILBERT

★

© 1967 by Editions d'Art Albert Skira, Geneva
Library of Congress Catalog Card Number: 66-30306

★

Distributed in the United States by
THE WORLD PUBLISHING COMPANY
2231 West 110th Street, Cleveland 2, Ohio

★

PRINTED IN SWITZERLAND

CONTENTS

THE AWAKENING

Western Europe was thinly, very thinly, populated in the year 1000. Great tracts of waste-land extended west, north and east, growing ever larger until they covered the entire face of this part of the continent: a seemingly endless wilderness of fens and forests, moors and winding rivers, bogs and copses, and the ragged undergrowth that springs up after forest fires and the operations of nomadic charcoal burners. At long intervals were clearings where, exceptionally, patches of land had been brought under cultivation, if only to a limited extent: shallow, irregular furrows cut in a stubborn soil with wooden plough-shares drawn by half-starved oxen. Even in the food-producing areas there were still large empty tracts, fields left fallow for a year, two years, even three, so that the soil could rest and gradually recover its fertility.

The men who worked the land lived in ram-shackle huts made of stone, mud or branches, surrounded by thorn fences and gardens. Some-times in the center of a group of huts protected by a palisade was the residence of a chieftain, with a wooden hall, granaries, sheds for the serfs and, a little way off, the hearth for cooking. Cities were few and far between and where one existed all that remained was the gaunt anatomy of a Roman town, mostly in ruins and ploughed over, a crumb-ling city wall, stone buildings dating to the Empire converted into churches or strongholds, and alongside them a huddle of vine-growers' huts and private houses occupied by priests and warriors, by weavers and the blacksmiths who manufactured weapons and articles of personal adornment for the garrison and the local bishop; also some families of Jewish money-lenders. Along the roads, now little more than cart-tracks, moved long files of carriers of merchandise and along the waterways whole fleets of boats. Compared with Byzantium or Cordova, the "cities" of the West cut a humble figure in the year 1000; poverty-stricken, fallen on evil times, haunted by the spectre of starvation.

Scanty though it was, the population was still, economically speaking, too large. The peasantry had to struggle, almost with their bare hands, against the enmity of nature, whose laws held them in thrall, and with a soil unrewarding for lack of expert tendance. For each grain of wheat he sowed no peasant expected to reap many more than three: just enough to provide his daily bread till Easter. After that he had to fall back on herbs and roots, the makeshift food procurable in forests and on the river banks. In the period of most arduous toil, the summer, the countryfolk had to work themselves to the bone, on empty bellies, nursing frail hopes of a plenteous harvest. But if it was a bad season—and many seasons turned out bad—there was a still earlier shortage and the bishops were constrained to relax ecclesiastical discipline and waive the rule against eating meat in Lent. Sometimes, too, when an exceptionally heavy rainfall had made the earth too sodden for autumn ploughing, or storms had laid low and spoilt the crops, shortages of this kind developed into those widespread famines whose horrid consequences are described with brutal candor by so many chroniclers of the period. "People hunted each other, devoured one another, and many cut the throats of their fellow-men and gorged on human flesh, like wolves."

Were they exaggerating when they spoke of piles of corpses in the charnel-houses, of starving men with empty bellies who took to eating earth and even, on occasion, digging up the bodies of the dead to allay the pangs of hunger? If these writers, all of them clerics, were at such pains to describe these tragic happenings and the great epidemics which decimated an undernourished populace and led to outbreaks of mob violence, the reason surely was that such calamities brought vividly home to them both the fragility of human life and the enigma of God's ways to man. To eat one's fill all the year round was a privilege reserved to members of the nobility and to a handful of priests and monks. All the others were enslaved to hunger and these writers saw in hunger an ineluctable concomitant of the human condition. Man, they thought, is born to suffering; he has a feeling of being naked, bare to the buffetings of fate, doomed to death, disease and daylong apprehension because he is a sinner. Since Adam's fall he has been the prey of hunger and no one can hope to be rid of it any more than of original sin. The men of that age lived in constant fear, not least of their own shortcomings.

Yet for some time already this early medieval world had been involved in an almost imperceptible movement that was delivering it little by little from abject poverty, and the eleventh century witnessed the gradual emergence of the peoples of western Europe from a state of barbarism. They were becoming less exposed to famine, achieving one by one a place in history, making steady headway towards a better mode of life. This was a period of awakening: the childhood of our civilization. For this part of the world—and this was to be its distinctive privilege, the mainstay of its growing ascendancy—was gradually entering on a period of immunity from invasions. Until now, for many centuries, wave after wave of migrant races had swept across the West, playing havoc with men's lives, destroying everything that lay on their path. True, the widespread conquests of Charlemagne had succeeded in restoring for a while a semblance of peace and order, but after the Emperor's death there was no resisting the hordes of invaders pouring in on all sides; from Scandinavia, from the eastern steppes, and from the Mediterranean islands overrun by the hosts of Islam, all of whom harried and pillaged Latin Christendom. The rude beginnings of what is known as Romanesque art make their appearance at the very time when invasions of this kind came to an end, in the regions where the Norsemen settled and developed an ordered way of life, where the King of Hungary installed the Christian faith, and whence the Count of Arles expelled the Saracen marauders who controlled the Alpine passes and had recently held to ransom the Abbot of Cluny. After 980 we hear no more tales of plundered abbeys and bands of terrified monks roving the countryside, carrying with them their relics and treasures. From now on, when flames were seen rising on the outskirts of the forests, these had been kindled by peasants reclaiming land for cultivation, not by pillagers.

That some progress in agricultural skills had been made in the "dark age" of the tenth century seems certain (though we know little about it). Initiated in the vast domains of the monasteries, these improvements had begun to take effect in the surrounding countryside; from now on they gathered speed and thanks to them the peasants of the feudal period were equipped with more effective implements, better ploughs, better harness and, above all, iron ploughshares capable of turning up the ground more efficiently, rendering it more fertile, and coping with heavy soil hitherto left untilled. As a result the cultivated area gained on the waste-lands, old clearings were enlarged, new ones opened up, and the improvement in farming methods led to more abundant harvests. No explicit mention of these improvements is made in extant records of the period, but there are many indications of them and they lay at the origin of all the cultural developments of the eleventh century. The famine of 1033 whose harrowing tale is told in the *Historiae* of Rudolph Glaber, a Cluniac monk, was in fact one of the last of the great famines; thereafter food shortages were less disastrous and took place at longer intervals. Thanks to the extension of the cultivated areas and increased productivity the land could easily support a larger population and these men were more robust, less vulnerable to epidemics. Calamitous though it was in many ways, the year 1000 witnessed, we can see, the upsurge of a new, active and enterprising generation, forbears of those who for three crowded centuries were to pioneer the ascent of Europe. As Thietmar, Bishop of Merseburg, in Saxony, observes in his *Chronicon* for the period 908-1018, "when came the thousandth year after the birth of our Saviour Jesus Christ by the Blessed Virgin, a radiant dawn flooded the world with light."

But that dawn did not rise for all; a vast majority were to live for a long while yet in darkness, destitution, constant anxiety. Whether free men or serfs, the peasants still had nothing of their own and, though they suffered less from hunger, were oppressed, denied any hope of escaping some day from their hovels and bettering themselves—even if they succeeded in accumulating, penny by penny, over ten or twenty years, just enough to buy a small patch of land. For in that age the landed nobility held them in close subjection; as a result of the rights of exploitation and privileges possessed by the rulers, the social order formed a pyramid of several tiers, sealed off from each other, with at the apex an all-powerful élite. A few families, friends and relations of the monarch, owned everything: the soil, the oases of cultivation, the waste-lands around them, the hosts of slaves, the taxes and corvées due from the tenant farmers on the great estates, the means of making war, the rights of judging and condemning, all the highest posts in the Church and State. Clad in rich garments, bedecked with jewels, attended by a mounted escort, the nobles roved the countryside, laying hands on the few chattels of any value owned by the impoverished inhabitants. The nobles alone benefited by the influx of wealth due to improved methods of cultivation. This rigorously hierarchic social order, the centralization of power and prosperity in the hands of the nobles and a favored few provide the explanation of how it was that, despite the extremely slow growth of this rudimentary material culture, we find, nonetheless, a surprisingly rapid expansion of so many activities in so many fields during the last quarter of the eleventh century: the development of de-luxe industries, the urge to conquest that sped the warriors of the West in all directions, and last but not least the rebirth of western culture. Had the supreme authority of a small group of nobles and churchmen pressed less heavily on the masses of powerless workers, the forms of art illustrated in this volume would never have come into being in those vast empty spaces among a peasantry so primitive and backward, so poverty-stricken, so totally devoid of even the vestiges of a culture.

What is perhaps most remarkable in these works of art is their diversity, the exuberant inventiveness of the men who created them, and none the less their fundamental unity. Latin Christendom extended over an immense area; months were needed to traverse it from end to end, intersected as it was by obstacles of all descriptions and huge empty tracts isolating the populated zones from each other. Each province lived a life apart, free to cultivate its ethnic idiosyncrasies. For in the flux and reflux of the great migrations, when empires were founded and soon fell to pieces, cultural layers of very different natures were deposited in various parts of Europe—some of them still quite novel in a whole group of regions, and intermixing or superimposed along their frontiers. Moreover the tenth-century invaders had ravaged the West to an extent that greatly varied

from place to place, and here we have another reason for the remarkably large number of local variants existing in the year 1000.

Nowhere were these differences more noticeable than on the confines of the Latin world. North, west and east the Christian lands were encompassed by a zone of barbarism, where paganism still flourished. These were the regions which had formerly been overrun by Scandinavians, Danish and Norwegian sea-venturers and traders from Gotland. There was still an abundant maritime traffic plying on the rivers and along the estuaries. Though piratical attacks on shipping still were frequent, the feuds between rival tribes and clans were tending to die out, giving place to commercial dealings of a peaceful order. From the Saxon strongholds in England, from the banks of the Elbe, from the forests of Thuringia and Bohemia and from Lower Austria missionaries were sallying forth, destroying idols and erecting crosses. Many died a martyr's death, but the princes of these lands, whose inhabitants were leading now more settled lives, building villages and installing farms, encouraged their subjects to be baptized and with the Christian faith to acquire a modicum of civilization. But the outlying, still semi-barbarian regions contrasted sharply with the southern marches, those of Italy and the Iberian peninsula, where contacts with Islam and Byzantine Christendom, far from primitive cultures, were operative. In the county of Barcelona, in the small kingdoms that had struck root on the mountains of Aragon, Navarre, Leon and Galicia, by way of the centers of culture in the Po delta, at Ferrara, Comacchio, Venice and above all Rome—frontier city between Hellenism and Latinity, always eyeing Constantinople with jealous admiration—a ferment of progress was creeping in. Along with new skills and new ideas, finely wrought objects were finding their way into these lands and, no less alluring, the gold coinage which testified to the material supremacy of the cultures on the frontiers of the southern zone of Latin Christendom.

Even in the heart of the vast area of Europe that Charlemagne had succeeded in incorporating in his empire, we find a great diversity. The most radical divergences, those that affected even the tenor of daily life, were determined by the greater or less extent to which Roman influences had made good their ascendancy. In some places, as in northern Germany, they seem wholly absent. Elsewhere they had been partially but not completely wiped out long ago by the inroads of barbarians, as was the case in Bavaria and Flanders. Elsewhere, again, they still were active and effective, as in Provence and, south of the Alps, in those lands where the towns were less dilapidated and where the native languages had a definitely Latin accent. Other contrasts, too, derived from the imprints left here and there by various races which during the early Middle Ages had settled in the West. The names of the lands they occupied betray their presence—Lombardy, Burgundy, Saxony, Gascony—and memories of the conquests of their ancestors in earlier times had developed a sense of nationality, premature in this age, among the provincial aristocracy. Associated with this was that rooted antipathy for "foreigners" which led the Burgundian chronicler Rudolph Glaber to mock the Aquitanians when one day he saw their troops escorting a princess. In the tangled pattern of the map of western Europe in the year 1000, the chief points of interest for the present-day historian are the regions where divergent cultures came in touch with each other, exchanged ideas and pooled discoveries, to the advantage of all concerned. Among these favoured regions were Catalonia and Normandy, the district of Poitiers, Burgundy, Saxony and the great plain stretching between Ravenna and Pavia.

More remarkable, however, is the deep-seated unity which prevailed at all cultural levels—notably that of creative art—in a civilization so widely scattered over an area so hard to bring under any uniform control. One reason for this underlying kinship was the extreme mobility of the population. For the most part it was congenitally nomadic, and this applies particularly to its higher ranks. Kings, princes, nobles, bishops and the large retinues which always accompanied them were continually on the move and made a point of visiting all their domains in the course of the year so as to consume their products on the spot and to hold their courts; moreover, hardly had they arrived than they set out to visit some local shrine or to lead a military foray. They lived on horseback, on the roads, and ceased their peregrination only in the dead of winter. Probably the worst privation for the monks was that of being confined, year in, year out, in a cloister; many of them found this unbearable and were accordingly permitted to move about, to change from abbey to abbey. Naturally enough these migra-

tory habits of the privileged élite on whose patronage all creative art depended led to fruitful contacts, rewarding exchanges of ideas.

No true frontiers existed in this part of Europe, divided up into small compartments. Once a man quitted the village where he had been born and bred, he was conscious of being a stranger everywhere and as such a suspicious character, in daily peril of robbery or worse. Adventure began on his doorstep and life was equally dangerous whether he settled a stone's throw from home or went to some remote country. Can one even speak of a frontier separating Latin Christendom from the rest of the world? In Spain no clear-cut barrier had ever existed between the zone in Moslem occupation and the regions ruled by Christian kings. The area of these latter fluctuated greatly as a result of the changing fortunes of war. In 996 Al-Mansur sacked Compostela, but fifteen years later the Count of Barcelona entered Cordova. Many petty Moslem princes were bound to the kings of Aragon and Castile by treaties under which they were assured protection and required to pay tribute. Conversely, a great number of active Christian communities flourished under the domination of the caliphs. Strung out in a continuous line along the Mediterranean coast then in Moorish occupation, from Toledo to Carthage, Alexandria and Antioch, these communities acted as connecting links between the western empire and Byzantium. All these factors must be taken into account when we seek to understand why Coptic themes proliferated so extensively in Romanesque iconography, and whence came the curious idiom of the illuminations in the Saint-Sever *Apocalypse* or the colonnettes and arches of Saint-Michel-de-Cuxa. For in point of fact eleventh-century Europe was less divided into water-tight compartments than it might seem at first sight to have been, and lent itself to exchanges of aesthetic ideas from country to country, race to race.

Among the various factors of cohesion operative at the higher cultural levels the Carolingian "cement" still played a vital part. For some decades practically all the West had been united under a single political domination, that of an homogeneous group of bishops and legislators, all of whom were members of the same families and had been educated under the aegis of the royal household. They held periodical meetings presided over by their common master, the monarch, and their many ties of kinship were strengthened by shared memories of their collective studies. This is why, widely scattered though it was, and despite natural obstacles, the aristocracy of the eleventh century formed a coherent whole, a body of men united in the same faith, by the same rites, the same language and the same cultural heritage. United, too, by abiding reminiscences of Charlemagne, that is to say of the immemorial prestige of Rome and the Roman Empire.

Yet even the most deep-seated affinities, those which did most to ensure a close cohesion between the various manifestations of art, were conditioned above all by the single *purpose* of that art. For in that age the sole mission of what we now call art was to offer to God worthy images of the visible world, His creation, and by such gifts to appease His wrath and win His favor. Thus every work of art was essentially numinous, not to say sacrificial, less concerned with aesthetics than with magic. Here indeed we have the most distinctive feature of the creative art of the period 980 to 1140. The expanding economy of this period, leading as it did to progress in many fields, provided Latin Christendom with the material means of creating less uncouth, far more advanced works of art, though this advance had not yet been carried far enough wholly to override

the mental attitudes and primitive comportment of the past. The eleventh-century Christian always felt himself overwhelmed by the mystery of things, a helpless puppet of the unseen, elemental, terrifying forces of the world that lay behind appearances. Even the best thinkers were haunted by phantasms of the irrational. This is why at this turning point of history, this brief interval in which, without yet being delivered from his dread of the unknown, man set to forging weapons to overcome it, there emerged the greatest and indeed the only truly sacred art of Europe.

Since this art was, as set forth above, an act of cult, a "sacrifice," it was under the exclusive control of those members of the community whose function it was to parley with the unseen powers governing life and death. In virtue of an ancient tradition this function had been vested in the king. But Europe was becoming feudalized; the power of the kings was disintegrating, passing into other hands. As a result, superintendence of the work of art was ceasing to be a royal prerogative. It was the monks who took it over, since in the existing climate of culture they were the most trusted intermediaries between man and the divine. And practically all the changes that came over the art of the West during this period reflect this gradual transference.

I

DESTINY
OF IMPERIAL ART

CROWN OF THE EMPEROR OTTO I. REICHENAU (?), ABOUT 962. KUNSTHISTORISCHES MUSEUM, VIENNA.

THE KINGS OF THE EARTH

"One alone reigns in the Kingdom of Heaven, He who hurls the thunderbolts; it is but natural that there should also be one alone who, under Him, reigns on earth." And in the eleventh century the world of men was commonly regarded as an image or reflection of the City of God, a city governed by a king. In fact feudal Europe could not dispense with monarchs, and when the crusaders, perhaps the most undisciplined army that has ever existed, swept down on the Holy Land, they promptly made of it a kingdom. Paragon of earthly perfection, the *persona* of the monarch invariably figured at the summit of all the mental diagrams which aspired to illustrate the order of the visible universe. Arthur, Charlemagne, Alexander, David—all the heroes of chivalric culture were kings, and it was with the king that every man, priest, warrior, even peasant, sought to identify himself. This permanence of what might be described as a mystique of royalty must not be lost sight of, for in it we have one of the predominant characteristics of medieval civilization. The conception of the work of art, in particular, was closely bound up with the idea of kingship, its functions and prerogatives. That is why, when seeking to elucidate the relations between the social system and creative art, we must begin by examining attentively the then accepted concept of royal power and the manner in which it functioned.

Kingship was a legacy of the Germanic past, brought by the races whom perforce the Romans had incorporated in their empire, without in the least subtracting from the powers of their rulers. The principal duty of these rulers was to lead their armies in battle, and every year when winter ended the young warriors mustered for some military exploit under their command. Thus throughout the Middle Ages the sword was chief of the emblems of sovereignty. But these barbarian kings had another prerogative, more numinous and still more vital to the common good: the magical power of interceding between the people and their gods; the welfare of the race depended on their mediation. This power came to them directly from the All Highest; divine blood ran in their veins and "the custom of the French was always, on the death of their king, to chose another member of the royal line." In this capacity the king presided at religious ceremonies and the chief sacrifices were made in his name.

An event momentous for its bearing on the "royal" art of Europe in the years to come took place in the middle of the eighth century. From then on the crowning of the mightiest of the monarchs of the West, accepted by all as the dominant figure of Latin Christendom, was a religious ceremony, like the coronations of the petty kings of northern Spain. In other words, he no longer owed his charisma to a mythical kinship with the obscure powers of the heathen pantheon; it was conferred on him directly by the Christian God, in the rite of sacring. When the priest anointed him with the holy oil he was invested with otherworldly powers and something of the sanctity of godhead. The king himself became a priest, ranking beside the bishops, who were consecrated with the same rites. *Rex et sacerdos*, he was given the ring and staff, insignia of a pastoral mission. By the hymns of praise chanted in the coronation ceremony the Church installed him in the heart of the celestial hierarchy. She defined his function, not merely that of a leader in the battlefield, but also that of a dispenser of peace and justice. Last and not least, since in the eighth century the art traditions stemming from the golden age of Rome survived in the West only under the aegis of the Church, and since all the architectural and decorative activities which hitherto had glorified the cities celebrated the glory of God—since in short all great art was now liturgical—it followed that the king, who by reason of the Christianization of his talismanic powers had become the leading figure in Church ritual, initiated and directed the major artistic enterprises. The rite of sacring had in effect transposed art into the royal domain.

The art forms due to monarchical initiative were given a more specific shape when, after 800, the restoration of the Empire had enlarged the scope of royalty. Imperial authority now became another divine institution ranking somewhat higher than before in the hierarchy of powers, midway between the kings of the earth and the celestial principalities. A pope had made obeisance to Charlemagne and on St Peter's tomb hailed him "Augustus." A Constantine redivivus and a new David, the Emperor of the West was charged with the task of guiding Latin Christendom on the path of salvation. On a page of a liturgical book, illuminated at Regensburg in 1002-1014, a painter depicted the Emperor Henry II in the center of a cruciform composition, i.e. at the "crossroads" of the universe, with angels coming down from heaven to invest him with the emblems of his sovereignty. St Ulrich and St Emmeram are uplifting his arms as Aaron and Hur held up the hands of Moses in the battle with the Amalekites and, throned in glory as in the Apocalyptic visions, Christ Himself is placing on his brow the diadem. Even more unequivocally than the kings who bowed down to them, the new emperors of the West saw themselves as God's vicegerents on earth. But they also knew themselves to be the successors of Caesar and in the acts of consecration they were called on to perform and which gave rise to works of art they were mindful of their forerunners, those whose largesse had embellished the cities of classical antiquity. Therefore they wished the objects presented to God at their bidding to bear the mark of a distinctive aesthetic, that of the Empire, in other words of Rome. Henceforth, and more deliberately than in the past, the artists who carried out their orders and those employed by the other sovereigns of the West drew inspiration from the masterpieces of Antiquity. All that in this eleventh-century art still shows affinities with the classicism of ancient Rome stems directly from the second rebirth of the western Empire.

For, two centuries after the coronation of Charlemagne as Emperor, creative art was still to a large extent oriented by the convergence of all temporal powers on the person of a sovereign, the Lord's Anointed, whose authority had a supernatural source and whose ministry, as set forth in the *Laudes Regiae*, signified the alliance of the two worlds, seen and unseen, the "cosmic harmony" between the earth and heaven. In the year 1000,

though the process of feudalization was steadily gaining ground, Europe continued to delegate to its emperor and its kings, its spiritual guides, the duties of rendering to God the homage of the people and of distributing among them the favors He bestowed. Similarly, there fell to them the task of tending the major offerings of the community, the churches, and providing the altar decorations, the reliquaries and the illuminated books in which God's words were enshrined. All agreed that these services befitted their high estate; that liberality, generosity, magnificence were attributes of kingship. By common consent the sovereign was *ex officio* a giver—to God and man—and works of beauty should flow from his open hands. Since, in the highly primitive social conditions of the age, the chief object of the gift was to dominate its recipient, to subject him to the donor, it was by making offerings that the monarch procured for his people the good will of the heavenly powers, and by his benefactions that he won the love of his people. When two kings met, each wished to prove himself the greater by the peculiar excellence of his gifts. This is why the leading artists of the eleventh century attached themselves to the monarchs—so long as these retained their power. The art of the age is essentially aulic, because it is a sacred art. Its best exponents operated in workshops under the patronage and control of the royal courts; indeed a geographic survey of eleventh-century art gives us an accurate idea of the respective eminence of the various kings of Europe.

In the year 1000 the most active creative centers in the West were to be found—as at Byzantium and in the Islamic lands—in the propinquity of the man who was regarded as the religious leader: in the case of Latin Christendom the Emperor. Reduced to a mere shadow of itself by the swift collapse of Charlemagne's successors, the imperial power had recovered substance and driving force in the land that the Carolingians had shaped with their own hands and civilized throughout its length and breadth: in Germania. This rejuvenation had begun in Saxony, most barbarous but also most vigorous of the German provinces, the one which had been spared by the hordes of marauders then scouring Europe, by reason of its extreme poverty, but also of the courageous resistance put up by the population. It was in Saxony that the fugitive monks took refuge, bringing with them their sacred relics and their skills. In the early tenth century the Saxon Dukes built fortresses at the foot of the Harz mountains, which proved an effective barrier against the onsets of the heathens, and the Germanic peoples chose one of these sturdy warriors to be their king. One of them won an epoch-making victory in Hungary which put an end to the invasions. Hailed as the saviour of Christendom, Otto soon became the protector and reformer of the Holy See. He was crowned emperor by the pope in 962 and, for the second time, the Empire was restored.

The Ottonian empire was more "Roman" than the Carolingian had been. In 998 Otto III, fourth of the line, decided to make his residence in a palace he had built on the Aventine and, though the *bulla* he used to seal his decrees still bore the effigy of Charlemagne, it had on the other side an image of the Eternal City, Roma Aurea. When speaking of himself and citing the long list of his titles, it was the honorific "Roman" that he placed in the forefront. And in pursuance of this *renovatio imperii romani* he spoke of Rome as "capital of the world." For the reborn Roman Empire boasted of its universality, and even more insistently than their predecessors its new masters claimed to be lords of the universe. Moreover there were now no clashes with Byzantium; the western emperors married "Greek" princesses and made no secret of their admiration for the Constantinople of the year 1000 where, too, a renaissance was in progress. It was from the Basileus that they took their new conception of imperial authority and the emblems of their power: the golden cope and the globe that fitted perfectly into the emperor's hand and signified a sovereignty embracing the entire world. At the chief State ceremonies Henry II (the "Saint") wore a great cloak whose embroidery invested his body with the constellations of the cosmos. As for the imperial crown (the one in the Vienna Museum may be that of Otto I), its eight sides, resembling the eight walls of the palatine chapels, signified eternity and symbolically evoked the heavenly Jerusalem, in other words the realm of perfection which would take form on the Last Day. Indeed it may well have seemed that the reign of the new Caesar prefigured that of Christ when at the end of Time He would return to take His throne on earth as King of Kings. The Ottonian emperors dreamed of making theirs once more a worldwide empire like that of God, and when giving their court painters commissions for illuminated liturgical books, often asked them to portray a group of large female figures, signifying the nations of the West, and they were shown bowing their heads in token of submission at the foot of the imperial throne.

Yet, in practice, the Emperor was unable to hold his own in Rome, where the old nobility entrenched in its ruined ancestral homes retained its ascendancy. He was king of Italy, and soon became king of Burgundy and Provence as well. But he reigned effectively only over the Germanic lands and Lotharingia, home of the lineage of Charlemagne. In the year 1000 Otto III went to Aachen where, "being unsure of the exact spot where the bones of Charlemagne rested, he had the pavement of the church torn up in secret at the place where he supposed they were, and continued digging until he found them, sealed in a royal sarcophagus. Then the emperor took for himself the cross of gold hung round the dead king's neck and such parts of his vestments as had not decayed, and after this set all back in place, with the utmost reverence." According to another chronicler the remains of the first restorer of the Empire were exposed to public view, like the relics of saints, and "proved their potency by signs and wonders and noteworthy miracles." Thus the restored imperial power was grafted on to the Carolingian trunk, around which already legends of strange happenings had gathered. Nominally, it was Roman and worldwide; in reality it had become almost entirely Germanic and as a result of this far-reaching change in the structure of the Empire the seminal centers of creative art in the eleventh century were to be found in Saxony, in the Meuse valley and on the shores of the Lake of Constance. It was the German lands that propagated to most effect the Frankish traditions of monarchical art, of architecture, of the pictorial and plastic forms in which was fructified the heritage of the workshops of the year 800, reinvigorated by Byzantine models and a return to Roman sources. But since the Emperor's real power was restricted to a few provinces and he was not the only monarch, "royal" art was no longer concentrated at a single point as in Carolingian times, and we find it operative in other kingdoms, far from the seat of empire.

For other kings were competing with the Roman and Germanic Caesars for the imperial title, to begin with those in the regions which Charlemagne had never subjugated. The English king styled himself "Totius Albionis Imperator Augustus." When in the early eleventh century Canute had extended his dominion over all the coasts of the North Sea and "five kingdoms had been brought under his sway: Denmark, Anglia, Brittany, Scotland and Norway," he had become an emperor. Similarly the kings of León, consecrated guardians of the shrine of Santiago de Compostela, after their many victories over the princes of Cordova, spoke of their *imperium* over the other Iberian kings. Lastly, in the very heart of Carolingian territory there still existed a king, but only one, whom his biographers thought fit to invest with the rank of an Augustus. For them the true Imperator Francorum was not the king of Germany but the ruler of West Francia, the king of France. In the year 1000 he was universally esteemed the chief rival of the Teutonic emperor; his bishops reminded him that "the Empire itself had been constrained to bow to his predecessors." Moreover the king of Germany treated him as an equal; when in 1023 the Emperor Henry II and King Robert of France met on the frontier of their respective dominions to discuss affairs of State, they greeted each other as brothers. By common consent the western world was split between two great kingdoms, one governed by the "Caesar," the other by the legitimate descendant of Clovis, the king who had been crowned at Reims beside that baptismal font at which in earlier days the people of the Franks had solemnized their pact with God. "We see that the Roman Empire has been, in the main, destroyed, but so long as there are Frankish kings with a vocation to preserve it, its glory will not wholly fade, since the kings will sustain it." Was it not clearly in favor of the Franks that the transfer of the *imperium* had taken place and was not the Ile-de-France the true Francia? Like Charlemagne, the Capetian monarch in the year 1000 held conclaves surrounded by bishops and counts, he embellished churches with his gifts, and the illuminations of sacred texts were made at his behest in abbeys under his patronage, at Saint-Germain-des-Prés and Saint-Denis in France. And since he felt himself heir to the Empire, the artists he employed (like those of Germany) used as their models the imperial works of the ninth century.

The *imperium*, the power of dispensing peace and justice, the sacred task of intercession and the cultural prerogatives allied with it were thus divided in the West in 1000. The effect of this was the rapid emergence of two Europes. One, that of the South, was kingless; for in the region beyond the Loire, including Catalonia, the French king's writ did not run. The authority of the Emperor as well was purely illusory at Lyons and in Provence, and in Italy, too, it was waning. Hence the opportunity in these southern provinces for the development of an art untrammelled by monarchical control. The European kingdoms were all located in the North, except for those in the highlands around León and Jaca in Spain, ruled by Christian sovereigns. On the fringes of the Europe of the kings, in the Scandinavian hinterlands and the isolated regions hemmed in by marshes where the first cathedrals of Poland, Bohemia and Moravia were now being built alongside the princely residences, serf artisans were continuing to employ for the personal adornments of the chieftains of tribes, who scarcely knew even the name of Christ, an art language stemming from the prehistoric past. Yet even here, thanks to progressive Christianization, the renown of a royalty consecrated by the Church was encouraging them to draw on reminiscences of the Carolingian aesthetic. This was what happened at Winchester under the approving eye of the Anglo-Saxon kings. And the Capetians made still more brilliant use of Carolingian art at Reims, Orléans and Chartres. But its true home was Germany. This was the chief source of all the forms of royal art which kept nearest to the spirit of Antiquity; they flourished in the forests of Saxony and most vigorously around Aachen, at Liège, on the banks of the Rhine, at the heart of what had been the Carolingian domain, and under the auspices of Henry II Bamberg (in Franconia) became their chief seminal center. The Teutonic emperors' frequent progresses through their dominions made that art known as far afield as Rome. These, in fact, were the places where, on the eve of the eleventh century, north of Tours, Besançon and the Alpine passes, the tradition of the Augustan patronage of art and the last traces of classical antiquity still survived, converted henceforth to the service of the Christian God.

THE EMPEROR

The Empire was the myth whereby the West, disrupted by the rise of feudalism, regained the basic unity of which it dreamt and which it deemed agreeable to God's plan. Under the imperial government, it became a united body, a brotherhood which, under the banner of Christ, advanced in serried ranks towards the promised bliss of the Heavenly City. This conception was bound up with the eschatological mystique which bulked so large in Christian thinking of the period. The end of the world and "the consummation of the Empire of Rome and of the Christians" were to take place conjointly when an emperor, last monarch of the age, came to Golgotha to offer his insignia to God—after which would come the reign of Antichrist. The imperium *envisaged in the eleventh century was a combination of three notions. Under its spiritual aspect it was a divinely appointed institution; the All Highest selected a ruler, gave him victory and by the same token filled him with his grace: that numinous power (*felicitas, Königsheil*) which set him above all other monarchs and made him the sole guide of God's people. It was on the battlefield, after their crushing defeats of the Hungarians, that first Henry the Fowler, then his son Otto I was acclaimed emperor by his troops, and both kings regarded themselves as Charlemagne's successors. Enduring memories of the Carolingian triumphs and the aura investing Aachen formed the second element of the "imperial idea" and this gave rise to a third: a belief that the defunct Imperium Romanorum had been reborn in the West. For the imperial myth was tied up with the Roman myth. The liturgical rites of the emperor's coronation could be solemnized only in the Eternal City, in the church erected on St Peter's tomb, and by the Bishop of Rome, and the sovereignty thus bestowed purported to be universal.*

This universality and its divine bestowal were given visual expression in a host of images: the dais (the throne on which Otto II took his seat as ruler of the nations of the world); the constellations and signs of the zodiac, signifying the firmament, woven on the cloak of Henry II; and the octagonal crown of the Holy Roman Empire. As "Servant of St Peter," the Emperor fulfilled an evangelical mission and by means of the missionaries he sent forth, sought to increase the number of believers. Before him was borne the Holy Lance containing one of the nails of the Cross. He led his people to the final triumph of good over evil, of resurrection over death. One symbol summed up all, a truly imperial symbol since it stood for victory, and that symbol was the cross: the cross that Otto III took from Charlemagne's neck, to hang it on his own; hence the countless crosses made by the court goldsmiths for the emperors, who distributed them as tokens of their invincible power.

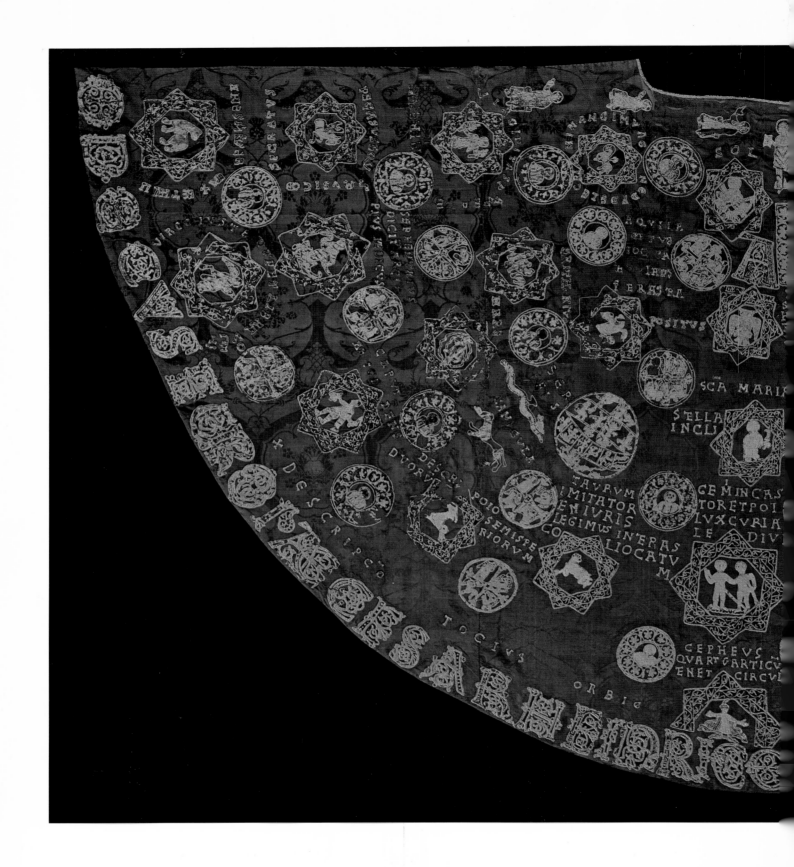

THE STAR-PATTERNED CLOAK OF THE EMPEROR HENRY II.

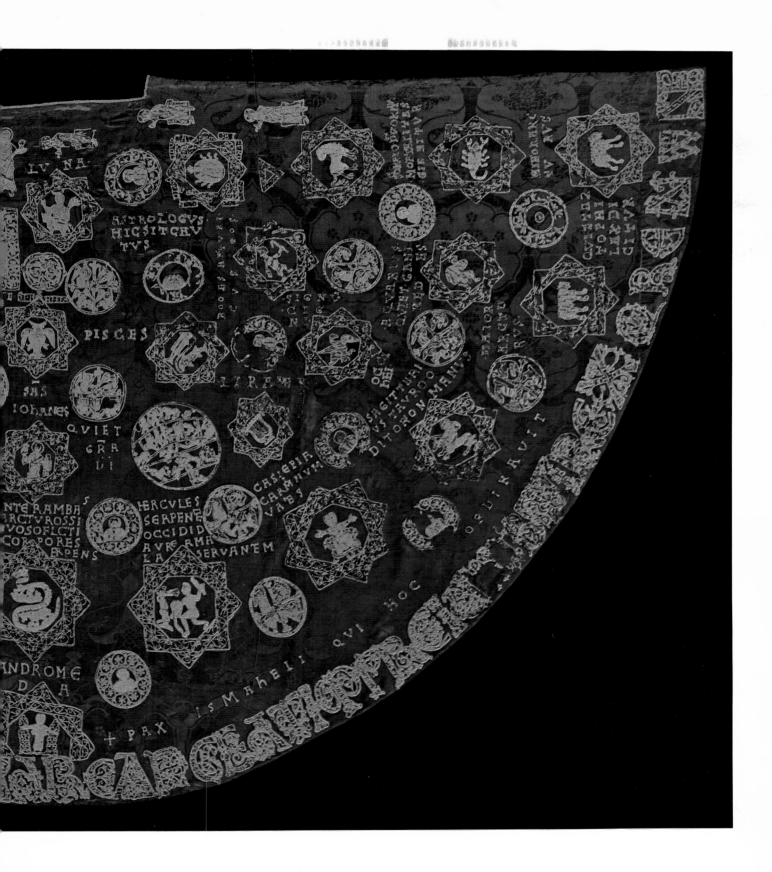

NORTH ITALY OR GERMANY (?), ABOUT 1020. DIOCESAN MUSEUM, BAMBERG.

LAMBERT OF SAINT-OMER, LIBER FLORIDUS: AUGUSTUS, RULER OF THE WORLD.
ABOUT 1120. FOLIO 138 VERSO, MS 92, UNIVERSITY LIBRARY, GHENT.

22

SO-CALLED CROSS OF LOTHAIR. COLOGNE, LATE 10TH CENTURY.
CATHEDRAL TREASURE, AACHEN.

MASTER OF THE REGISTRUM GREGORII: THE EMPEROR OTTO II WITH THE SYMBOLS
OF THE FOUR PARTS OF HIS EMPIRE. TRIER, ABOUT 983. MUSÉE CONDÉ, CHANTILLY.

THE KING AS CHRIST

The imperial administration did not make an end of kings; royalty was an older institution and no less sacrosanct. The king, too, believed himself a Christ. Like the bishops, shepherds of the people and successors of the apostles, he owed his rank to an intervention of the Holy Ghost, was acclaimed by an assemblage of churchmen and warriors in a cathedral and anointed with holy oil which bestowed on him the power of vanquishing evil. Describing the coronation of the German king, Bishop Otto of Freising wrote as follows: "On the same day and in the same church, the elected bishop of Münster was consecrated by the same prelates who had anointed the king, so that the presence of both the king and the supreme prelate at the ceremony might be regarded as a favorable presage for the future, since the same church and the same day witnessed the unction of the two persons who, as enjoined in the Old and New Testaments, are the only persons sacramentally anointed, each alike entitled Christus Domini." *The king, that war-lord whose* potestas *ended once age or infirmity had made him incapable of riding a horse, was also a member of the priesthood. The one man in the Christian community whose power lay at the junction between the spiritual and the temporal, on the border of the seen and unseen worlds, he was minister of both the sacred and the secular. Helgaud of Saint-Benoît-sur-Loire, who wrote the life of King Robert of France, describes him as "a man of God" whose chief function, like the monks', was praying for his people. "So devoted was he to the Scriptures that never a day passed without his reading the Psalms and beseeching the Most High in the words of St David." The vow made on the day of his sacring imposed on him the duty of protecting "God's people" (the priests and the poor) against the powers of darkness. When the members of his court were seated at his feet, he occupied the same place as Jesus, whom the age envisaged primarily as a crowned judge. Like Jesus, the king had a miraculous power of curing diseases. "By the will of God," Helgaud continues, "this perfect man had so wonderful a gift of healing that if he laid his very pious hand on the place where a disease was lurking, he cured it then and there." Despite the fact that Henry IV, King of Germany, had been excommunicated, peasants flocked to him, when he was traveling through Tuscany, so as to touch his garment, believing this would ensure for them better harvests. Thus "the king holds a place above the common herd of laymen, for being anointed with the holy oils he participates in the sacerdotal ministry," and in the eyes of God is the supreme sacrificer. This explains the part he played in creative art, always envisaged in this age as an offering to God and an act of consecration.*

NEW MINSTER CHARTER: KING EDGAR OF ENGLAND (957-975) PRESENTING THE CHARTER TO GOD.
WINCHESTER, 966. FOLIO 2 VERSO, COTTON VESP. A. VIII, BRITISH MUSEUM, LONDON.

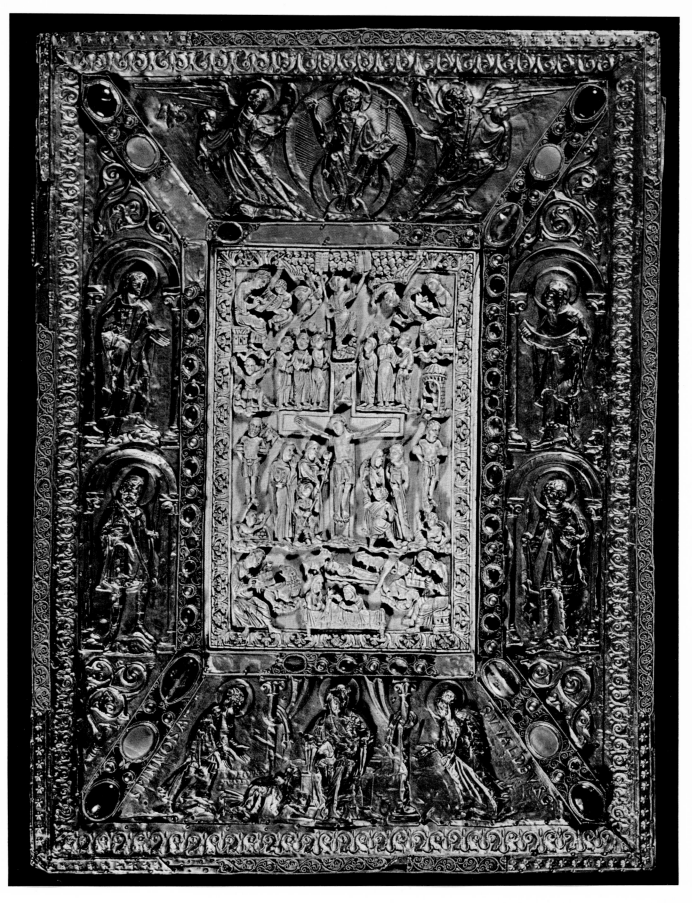

IVORY COVER OF THE GOSPEL BOOK OF ABBESS THEOPHANU OF ESSEN (1039-1056): THE CRUCIFIXION.
MID-11TH CENTURY. CATHEDRAL TREASURE, ESSEN.

GOSPEL BOOK OF OTTO III: THE SERMON ON THE MOUNT. REICHENAU, 1010.
FOLIO 34 VERSO, CLM. 4453, STAATSBIBLIOTHEK, MUNICH.

CHRIST THE KING ENTHRONED IN THE CITY OF HEAVEN. FIRST HALF OF THE 12TH CENTURY.
FRESCO IN THE VAULT OF THE NARTHEX, CHURCH OF SAN PIETRO AL MONTE, CIVATE, NEAR COMO.

ANGLO-SAXON SACRAMENTARY: THE NATIVITY. ELY, 1006-1023. FOLIO 32 VERSO, MS Y.6, BIBLIOTHÈQUE MUNICIPALE, ROUEN.

The Carolingians had decreed that every cathedral and church in the Empire should have a school attached to it. During the eleventh century the schools in northern Christendom remained very much as they had been when Alcuin and his disciples established them two hundred years before. As a matter of fact the relative prestige of the educational centers was determined by the personality of the bishop of the diocese or the abbot of the local monastery. A stable element in almost every school was its collection of books, a source of knowledge that the scholasticus, *canon or monk in charge of studies, could consult for the courses he delivered. As it so happened, Carolingian copyists had stocked these libraries with classical works and they served to keep alive the humanist tradition.*

There was a natural link between the school proper and the scriptorium, the place where the copies of ancient texts were made. But in this period all books were regarded quite as much as adjuncts of the liturgy as vehicles of knowledge. And since the book played a not unimportant part in Divine Service it had to be decorated, like the altar, the sacred vessels and the walls of the church. It became an "object of art" in which the connection between the written culture and the image was given its most intimate expression. So it was that the tradition of ancient art was transmitted most effectively by the decorative work done in scriptoria. In the eleventh century prayer books, lectionaries and Bibles illustrated in the reigns of Louis the Pious and Charles the Bald were still to be found in all the monastic and cathedral libraries, and the aesthetic qualities of these works were appreciated and admired by clerics and laymen alike. The paintings in them were almost without exception imitations of Early Christian models. The plastic vigor of the evangelist portraits and the simulated architecture in which the figures were located, all the ornaments surrounding calendars and canon tables were attuned to the humanist ideal of the Latin poets and historians. Since these works, it seemed, transmitted the message of Augustan Rome and, like the teaching of the grammarians, inculcated the pure Latinity of an earlier age, untouched by barbarian solecisms, the images in Carolingian books inspired the same respect as the classical writers. They were copied, just as the texts of Virgil, Suetonius and Terence were copied. The artists who were commissioned by the emperor at Reichenau or Echternach and at Saint-Denis by the kings of France, to make paintings for the Gospel Books, drew freely on the imagery of the ninth-century illuminators so as to produce decorations appropriate to the dignity of their royal patrons. But they did not copy slavishly, their figurations tended to diverge from the Carolingian prototypes. Though given plain gold grounds signifying an abstraction from the temporal akin to the sense of the eternal conveyed by the liturgic rites, these images still conformed to the aesthetic of the Late Empire. Resolutely figural, they represented the human body as the eye sees it, located in space, without deliberately modifying its proportions.

A bolder forward step was the revival of relief work. True, Carolingian artists had drawn inspiration from Roman sculpture but usually in a somewhat timid manner; in the ninth century paganism was still a peril to be reckoned with. If statues of Our Lord and, more especially, of saints were publicly exhibited, was there not a risk of encouraging a rebirth of idolatry? This is why figures carved in ivory or moulded by goldsmiths were always placed beside the altar where they would be seen only by initiates and the officiating priests, by those whose faith and culture immunized them against temptation. But at the end of the tenth century this danger had ceased to exist; the wooden idols once worshipped by the tribes had long since been demolished, the Cross had triumphed, the Church had nothing to fear from pagan gods. So there was now no obstacle to placing representations of sacred personages, given the convincingness of full plasticity, on the doors of churches. First to make a move in this direction was, it seems, Bernward, Bishop of Hildesheim. A man of learning, he was employed by the Emperor as tutor to his son, but his biographers speak of him also as an architect, an illustrator of manuscripts, and a skilled metal-worker. For the monastery of St Michael which he had founded near his cathedral to serve as his burial place, he had two bronze doors cast, piece by piece, in 1015. In this he was following the example of Charlemagne and high prelates of the Carolingian Church. But he was the first to adorn church doors with images. Those at Hildesheim are covered with them. There are sixteen scenes set out one above the other in two parallel columns. On the left are Old Testament figures spanning the period from the Creation to the slaying of Abel; they illustrate the Fall. On the right is an ascending sequence of Gospel figures, from the Annunciation to the Resurrection, illustrating the process of redemption by which humanity rises to the celestial heights.

The Hildesheim doors marked a rebirth of large-scale relief work, and this took place, surprisingly enough, in one of the outlying, least civilized parts of the West. They were imitated in the Rhineland and the Meuse region. Thus the trail was blazed which, from the reliefs on the gold altar of Basel, led to the perfectly classical forms of those made by the bronze-founder Renier de Huy in 1107 on a baptismal font at Liège. Whether this wonderful renascence may have inspired the large-scale sculpture at Cluny is a moot point, but there is no question that it pointed the way to the revival of monumental statuary in the twelfth century, first at Saint-Denis, then at Chartres.

GOSPEL BOOK OF OTTO III: JESUS WEEPING OVER JERUSALEM. REICHENAU, 1010.
FOLIO 188 VERSO, CLM. 4453, STAATSBIBLIOTHEK, MUNICH.

THE CRUCIFIXION. LATE 11TH OR EARLY 12TH CENTURY. IVORY.
TREASURE OF THE CATHEDRAL OF SAINT-JUST, NARBONNE.

BRONZE DOOR OF BISHOP BERNWARD, UPPER LEFT HALF: SCENES FROM GENESIS. 1015.
CATHEDRAL OF HILDESHEIM.

35

"THE BASEL APOSTLES." FIRST QUARTER OF THE 12TH CENTURY. FRAGMENT OF AN ALTAR RELIEF.
BASEL CATHEDRAL.

GOLD ALTAR FRONTAL FROM BASEL CATHEDRAL. FIRST QUARTER OF THE 11TH CENTURY.
MUSÉE DE CLUNY, PARIS.

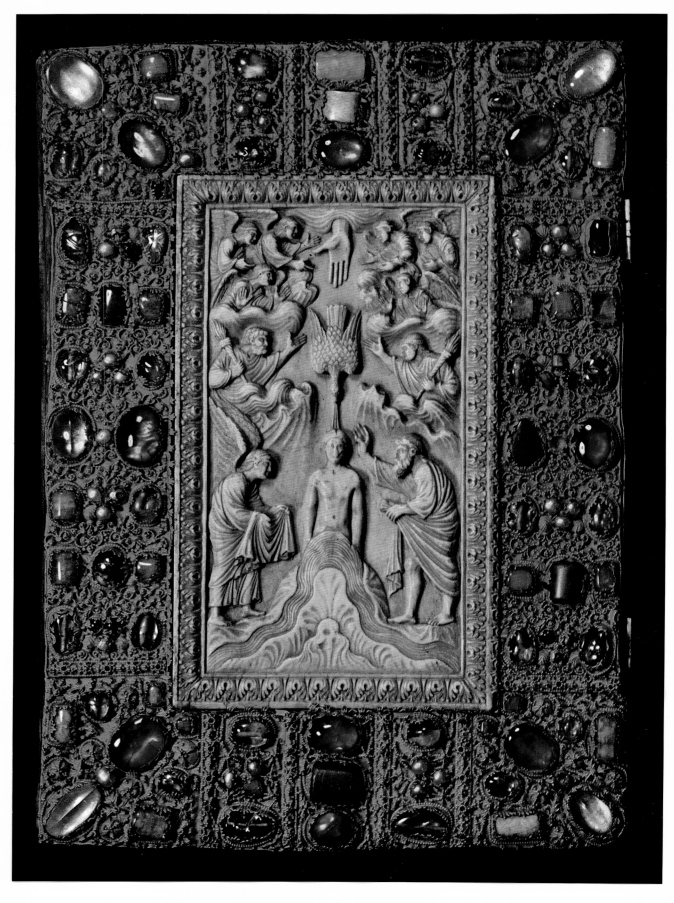

IVORY COVER OF A GOSPEL BOOK: THE BAPTISM OF CHRIST. WESTERN GERMANY, ABOUT 960-980.
CLM. 4451, STAATSBIBLIOTHEK, MUNICH.

BAPTISMAL FONT OF RENIER DE HUY. 1107-1118.
CHURCH OF SAINT-BARTHÉLEMY, LIÈGE.

ST AUGUSTINE, DE CIVITATE DEI: TITLE PAGE. CANTERBURY, ABOUT 1100.
FOLIO 2 VERSO, PLUT. 12, COD. 17, BIBLIOTECA LAURENZIANA, FLORENCE.

given their baptisteries this form, since in them took place the rites whose numinous virtue freed man from the shackles of the earth and enabled him to soar to the celestial heights where angels hymn eternally the praise of God. Clearly a similar plan was needed for the churches whence the sovereign launched prayers of intercession to the Almighty. Ottmarsheim, consecrated in 1049 by Pope Leo IX, imitated Aachen, as did so many churches then built in the Empire, even at its confines on the Slav frontier where Christianity, backed by the imperial army, was gaining ground. The central plan, with two superimposed elevations, also derived from an existing tradition, that of the martyrium or reliquary-tomb, transmitted by the builders of crypts. When at their journey's end pilgrims to the Holy Land came to Jerusalem, they entered a round church, built in the same manner as the Emperor's chapel.

However, once the Church had triumphed and Christianity, coming out of hiding, had invaded Rome and taken possession of its most official edifices, almost all Roman churches—especially the outstanding ones, those which were built above the tombs of St Peter and St Paul—were basilicas, that is to say "royal courts," large oblong buildings of the type used for judicial proceedings, with rows of arcades supporting a light wooden roof and dividing the interior into three parallel aisles. There was an apse equivalent to the seat of the Judex in pagan times, and ample lighting was provided by the tall windows of the central aisle. In fact, the internal arrangement of the House of God had much in common with an ancient forum. During the Carolingian period, owing to changes in the ritual, the church entrance had been modified, and the atrium roofed over so that it became a sort of vestibule or antechurch two storeys high, with a sheltered porch at ground level and a room for prayer above. Were these alterations intended to detain the crowds of pilgrims in the forepart of the church and prevent them from disturbing the services? Or to provide a special place for the worship of Christ the Saviour, who shared the patronage of the church with a local saint? Or was this enlargement of the portal due to the recent extension of funerary rites? Whatever the answer to these questions, it certainly lay at the origin of that solid mass of masonry which, throughout the Empire, gave the basilicas a second apse

JUMIÈGES (NORMANDY), CHURCH OF THE BENEDICTINE ABBEY. 1040-1067.

BARI (SOUTH ITALY), BASILICA OF SAN NICOLA. 1087.

SAINT-BENOÎT-SUR-LOIRE (NEAR ORLÉANS), NARTHEX OF THE CHURCH. 1004-1030.

1

THE BASILICA

Europe in the year 1000, for the building of her churches, had inherited from Carolingian culture two types of edifices, both of which claimed to conform to the Roman tradition at its purest. For more than any other kind of architecture the churches were treated as royal buildings since, for one thing, God was regarded as the crowned sovereign of the world seated on his throne to judge the living and the dead; and, secondly, because every place of worship was under the direct patronage of the king, Christ's vicegerent on earth. And since the kings of Europe regarded themselves as heirs of the Empire, it seemed right and proper that monuments due to their munificence and the peace reigning in their dominions should take inspiration from ancient Rome.

Charlemagne had wished his oratory at Aachen to resemble the imperial chapels, an example of which he had seen at Ravenna: a round church. The circular plan purported to symbolize the king's specific mission of interceding between his people and God, between the temporal and the spiritual, nature and supernature. For the design of this type of church embodied the connection between the square (sign of the earth) and the circle (sign of heaven); and in the symbology of numbers the octagon, which effected the transition between them, signified eternity. In Rome the Early Christians had

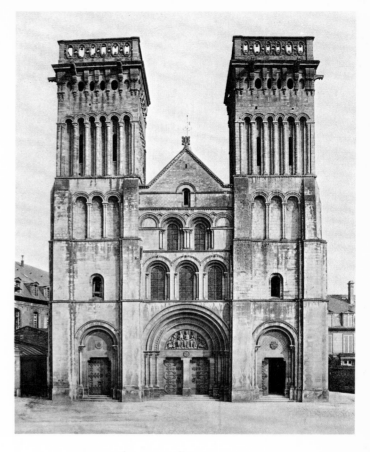

CAEN (NORMANDY), TRINITY CHURCH
OR ABBAYE AUX DAMES. FOUNDED IN 1062.

CAEN (NORMANDY),
CHURCH OF SAINT-ETIENNE
OR ABBAYE AUX HOMMES.
FOUNDED IN 1064.

CAEN (NORMANDY), ▶
INTERIOR OF TRINITY CHURCH
OR ABBAYE AUX DAMES.
FOUNDED IN 1062.

45

CÉRISY-LA-FORÊT (NORMANDY), INTERIOR OF THE ABBEY CHURCH, LOOKING TOWARDS THE APSE. LATE 11TH CENTURY.

at the west end corresponding to the belfry-porches at the entrance of churches in the Ile-de-France.

In the eleventh century these royal types of architecture prevailed in the north of western Europe, where monarchy best resisted the encroachments of feudalism. That is, north of the Alps, in all the provinces where the king of Germania had the bishops under his control: in Lotharingia, homeland of the first line of Christian "Caesars" in the West (the Carolingian princesses were buried in the crypt at Nivelles), and in Saxony, cradle of the second restorers of imperial dignity. The basilica at Gernrode, begun three years after the imperial coronation of Otto I, and St Michael's at Hildesheim, founded by Bishop Bernward, tutor of Otto III, where the bishop was buried (in the Chapel of the Cross) show complete fidelity to Carolingian models. These were also copied in Champagne, at Vignory, at Montier-en-Der, and the region of Reims provided a connecting link between the art of the Ottos and that of the Capetians. However, at this time little building was being done in the Ile-de-France, the only churches built shortly after 1000 being those for which King Robert had a special veneration: Orléans, Saint-Benoît-sur-Loire, Saint-Martin of Tours. Later, the art of Neustria came to florescence in the most prosperous, most solidly organized of the feudal States: the Duchy of Normandy. Its rulers had a predilection for the monasteries reformed by William of Volpiano; in 1037 the building of a new basilica began at Jumièges. On the eve of his conquest of England Duke William, to atone for a marriage condemned as incestuous by the Church, provided jointly with his wife the funds for building two abbey churches at Caen: that of the Trinity, begun in 1062, and St Stephen's, begun two years later. The innovations of the Neustrian architects were perfected in the Norman workyards; in the apse a line of radiating chapels flanked the ambulatory, the towers of the façade were prolonged by buttresses. These methods were propagated far afield in the wake of the great expeditions launched by the Norman knights. Not, however, as far as Bari, where the basilica was built in the Roman style. But in conquered England Norman architecture flowered, and Abbot Suger took inspiration from it when at Saint-Denis he built what was to be the prototype of the Gothic cathedral.

ROME: AN ABIDING PRESENCE

Eleventh-century man visualized his king as a horseman, sword in hand, dispensing peace and justice to his people. But he also saw in him a sage, and assumed he was capable of reading books. Once the western world had come to regard the monarchy as a *renovatio*, a rebirth of the imperial power, sovereigns could no longer remain illiterate, as their barbarian ancestors had been. The ruler was now expected to conform to the ideal image that Rome had built up of the "good emperor," paragon of knowledge and fount of wisdom. "In his palace he has a multitude of books, and when he chances to have a respite from warfare, he devotes it to reading them, spending long nights in meditation on their contents, until sleep seals his eyes." This commendable habit is attributed by a chronicler hailing from Angoulême to the Duke of Aquitaine, when he seeks to convince his reader that the Duke was the peer of kings. Before this, Einhard, friend and biographer of Charlemagne, had spoken of the emperor's persistent efforts to learn to write; King Alfred had had the Latin texts in monastery libraries translated into Anglo-Saxon so that the nobles of his court could understand them; and Otto III, emperor in the year 1000, had presided in person over the debates of men of learning and summoned the most famous, Gerbert (later Pope Sylvester II) to his court.

Nevertheless it was the coronation ceremony that did most to seal the alliance between the monarchy and erudition. For in virtue of this rite the sovereign was invested with a sacerdotal function, and it was the bounden duty of a priest to familiarize himself with books, now that the Word of God was inscribed in written texts. Thus the king had to be a "man of letters" and he saw to it that the son who was to inherit the crown received the education of a bishop. Hugh Capet, though he had not yet ascended the throne (but hoped to do so), put Robert, his eldest boy, to study under Gerbert, ablest pedagogue of the day, asking him to impart to Robert "sufficient knowledge of the liberal arts to make him acceptable to Our Lord by the practice of all the holy virtues." But it was also incumbent on the sovereign, responsible as he was for the salvation of his subjects, to see that the clergy, of which he now formed part, was qualified for its high vocation, in other words that it was well-educated. Hence his active support of institutions which, in a social order whose aristocracy, wholly militarized, had turned its back on studies, shaped ecclesiastics for their sacred calling. If today Charlemagne is pictured as a fatherly patron of schools, reprimanding bad pupils, patting the heads of good ones, this is because more than any other he applied himself to carrying out the duties of a Christian monarch. All reigning sovereigns of around 1000 followed his example. They saw to it that monasteries and cathedral churches were well supplied with books and teachers, and tried to establish in their residences the best possible educational centers. For among the many young scions of the aristocracy attached to the royal court, those who were not destined to a military career but to the Church had to be provided with the intellectual pabulum needed to qualify them for holding the highest posts, worthy of their rank, in the ecclesiastical hierarchy. The powers that God had delegated to his vicegerent, the sovereign, made this one of the latter's most immediate and urgent duties. Education was always closely involved with the monarchy in the eleventh century. And for two reasons: because the king regarded himself as the successor of the Caesars, and even more because, in St Jerome's translation of the Scriptures, God expressed Himself in the language of Augustus, the culture diffused by the royal schools was neither contemporary nor vernacular. That culture was, in fact, a heritage that successive generations had piously safeguarded through the darkness and decadence of the early Middle Ages: the heritage of a lost golden age, that of the Latin Empire. Essentially classical, it kept alive the memory of ancient Rome.

How many were there to benefit by this education? Some hundreds, possibly thousands, in each generation, and of these only a privileged few, perhaps several dozen in all, had access to the highest grade of knowledge. Though scattered all over Europe at very great distances from each other, these schoolmen knew each other, exchanged letters and manuscripts. They were the makings of the medieval "school"—they and the books they had copied with their own hands or been given by colleagues—and they attracted to them small groups of auditors, men of all ages who had often traveled half way across Europe, sometimes even risked their lives, to sit at the feet of the masters and hear them read or lecture. All were churchmen, all cultivated learning not for its own sake but so as the better to serve God and understand His words. The mother tongues of members of these groups differed completely from the language of the Bible and the liturgy. So a study of Latin words, their meanings and usages—the acquisition of a knowledge of the lexicon and grammar—was an essential part of the curriculum. The pedagogues of Late Antiquity had formulated seven ways to the getting of understanding, the seven so-called liberal arts, all of which figured in the scholastic program. But the eleventh-century teachers gave serious attention only to the first and most elementary, an initiation into the language of the Vulgate. "Students," wrote Abbon of Fleury in 1000, "must begin by learning to swim expertly in the deep, tumultuous, treacherous ocean of Priscian's *Grammar*; next, to make them grasp the meaning of Genesis and the Prophets, the teacher should read out to them and make them in turn read out such models of good Latinity as Virgil, Statius, Juvenal, Horace, Lucan and Terence." True, these writers were heathens, but they had handled the Latin language to perfection. That is why after the catastrophic end of Roman culture their works were rescued from oblivion. Parts of them had escaped destruction and, in view of their educational value, intensive search was made for these in the libraries that had suffered least—those of Italy—and these fragments were collated in the scriptoria attached to every teaching center. Young priests and novices copied out long extracts from these books and memorized them, and *disjecta membra* of classical poems came constantly to their lips, mingled with verses from the Psalms. As a result of these methods of education the highest dignitaries of the Church

developed into humanists, bent on imitating the best classical writers, and discreetly plagiarizing them. A German abbess, Hrosvitha, "adapted the plays of Terence so as to make them suitable reading for the sisters of her convent." Born in the purple, the Emperor Otto III was given the education of a cleric; he dispatched his scribes to Reims and the Abbey of Bobbio with orders to make copies of the works of Caesar, Suetonius, Cicero and Livy, so as to have a complete record of the glories of Republican and Imperial Rome, the Rome he dreamed of making once again the center of a worldwide empire, and at Pavia he spent long hours studying and musing on Boethius' *De Consolatione Philosophiae*. This, to his thinking, was one of the obligations of kingship. Thus the methods of teaching practised in the ecclesiastical schools, the whole trend of scholastic culture and its unflinching championship of Roman literary values maintained, at the dawn of the feudal age, a close association between the monarchical institution and ancient literature, the masterworks of Antiquity which the kings, as students, had been trained to revere and imitate. This explains why that part of the art activity of the eleventh century which emanated directly from the person of the sovereign drew so tenaciously on the classical heritage.

It was the taste for well-turned Latin poems and the cult of Antiquity resulting from it that led such a man as Bernward, Bishop of Hildesheim, and tutor of Otto III, to commission an imitation of Trajan's Column, to give his church bronze doors and to have their decorations made in a thoroughly classical style. For the heads of schools of which the sovereigns were patrons did not salvage merely classical texts, but all that had survived of ancient Rome. Its monuments were falling in ruins, but its cameos, ivories and the remains of its statues were reverently preserved. One day Abbot Hugh of Cluny received a poem celebrating the discovery at Meaux of a Roman bust. For the old mistrust of a taint of paganism lingering on in these stones and images was gradually dying out. The Christian faith was now so solidly established that it had nothing to fear from the idols which early missionaries had felt a compulsion to destroy and eleventh-century art lovers had no need to feel qualms about admiring these collectors' pieces evidencing the highly developed culture which had given birth to them. The teaching of the schoolmen dispelled illusions of their intrinsic "wickedness"; the Christian could take over the beauties of the pagan world provided he dedicated them to God. With the sovereigns' approbation grammarians took their examples from the classics and the creators of the new royal art drew inspiration from the same source.

This antiquizing tendency of the new monarchical art was encouraged by the fact that its workshops always functioned in the neighborhood of a church or palace treasure. The king, so lavish of gifts for the welfare of all his subjects, and thanks to whose munificence all the places of worship under his control were provided with precious stuffs and jewels, clad himself in rich garments, bedecked with ornaments, when he showed himself to his people. Since he was in God's image, was it not fitting he should thus adorn his person? This display of gems and gold invested his form with glory, and made visible to all the aura of divinity surrounding a Christian king. On the material side, these precious objects were tokens of his earthly power, they impressed his rivals; also, this parade of the wealth on which the sovereign could draw to reward his friends was a stimulus to loyalty. No king without a treasure—and when its lustre dimmed it meant that the royal power, too, was dwindling. Such collections had been gradually amassed over a long period, perhaps centuries. Some of the finest pieces were dynastic heirlooms, handed down generation by generation; others were gifts from eastern potentates. Nearly all bore the stamp of Rome; of the bygone Rome whose wonders barbarian kings had looted to adorn their pomps and ceremonies; or of the new, rejuvenated Rome at Byzantium where a renaissance, accompanied as it so happened by a revival of the ancient style, was now in progress. Lastly, these collections were by no means "dead"; they had nothing in common with a modern museum. They were put to daily use and since each object in them had a specific function in a culture where ceremony played a major part, all was conveyed by way of rites or symbols, each decoration, every adornment, every detail, was meaningful. Exchanges of gifts were constantly adding new pieces to the treasure. One of the principal duties of the artists attached to the royal household was to keep the king's treasure in good condition, to renovate old ornaments so that they could figure as accessories at religious or secular ceremonies, to perform such tasks as setting a cameo in the binding of a Gospel book or transforming an ancient cup into a chalice. Another of their duties was to modify newly acquired objects so as to bring them into line, as far as possible, with the other pieces in the treasure. In this mass of goldsmith's work classicizing trends predominated. So, naturally enough, with an eye to harmony no less than out of deference to an aesthetic tradition whose chief repositories were the royal residences, the palace artists did their best, in their renovations and adaptations, to achieve the technical perfection of ancient works of art. It was above all the stylistic principles of these works that they studied and adopted.

The same spirit prevailed in the libraries annexed to the study centers patronized by the sovereign; also in the sumptuous ornaments which proclaimed his wealth and power at the coronation festivities. For in the embellishments of Christian ceremonies use was often made of ancient motifs, examples of the beauties of a golden age of art, and objects on which these figured were carefully preserved or faithfully reproduced. Doubtless the artisans working for the kings in the eleventh century copied these prototypes less slavishly than their predecessors had done in the days of Charlemagne and during the first renaissance of imperial culture. For since Antiquity was now remoter by two centuries, and Carolingian copies were often all they had to go on, memories of it were losing precision and more latitude was allowed to the artist's personal inventiveness. However, the fact remains that basic to the best culture of this period was a thorough-going deference to the past, due to a keen sense of the relative barbarism of the present age. This discouraged any attempts at originality, any hope to vie with a perfection that had long since left the world. Like the prelates-to-be, like the kings who in their nightly vigils tried to learn to read, the goldsmiths, painters, artificers employed by the court saw themselves as the merest tyros; their one ambition was to assimilate their work as far as possible to Roman models and keep to the safe and beaten track of tradition. So it was that in the heart of a countryside covered with dense forests, in towns where herds of swine were the only scavengers, the kings were still surrounded by memories of the great age of Rome. Hence an aesthetic attuned to the prosody of the *Aeneid* and Lucan's *Pharsalia*: an art that ruled out imagination, the tortuous geometric abstractions of Germanic jewelry, the distortions of human and animal forms found on barbarian ornaments. It was essentially an art of words, discourse and dialogue, not of symbols or free fancy; an art of monumental forms, not of line and incised images, and its true exponents were architects and sculptors. Such in fact was the art of the "pericopes" that the Reichenau painters illuminated for the emperors; of the Saint-Denis scriptorium; of the baptismal fonts at Liège.

Reichenau, Saint-Denis and Liège were not capitals; the kings of that time had none. They were always on the move; their military duties forced them to be continually on horseback. However, their religious function obliged them sometimes to call a halt, when, like the bishops, they were due to take part in solemn celebrations of the chief festivals of the Christian year in the great churches. Nor was there ever any question of displacing the cultural centers, whose formation and activities they encouraged. The art schools and workshops were established in the great abbeys patronized by the monarch, under the aegis of the royal churches, and in the bishoprics on which his power largely reposed. Thus it is possible to draw up a map of the centers of education, a map that does not precisely coincide with the geographical distribution of the kingdoms, but, combined with this, accurately indicates the domain in which during the period we are dealing with the classical spirit continued to predominate.

This domain hinges on a region extending from the Loire to the Main, covering exactly the same area as that of the Carolingian renaissance. It was in the Frankish provinces, and in the entourage of the royal palaces, that Alcuin's work bore fruit and the teachers who sought to restore in ecclesiastical circles the usage of correct Latin, labored to best effect. Further east, Germania was a far less promising field for such endeavors. In the zone of German influence the only really active centers of learning were still, as in the days of Charlemagne, the monasteries of Franconia and those on the banks of the Rhine, Echternach, Cologne, St Gall; above all, the churches of the Meuse valley. On the borders of the provinces which had been wholly barbarized by the invasions of the early Middle Ages, and of those where the Roman imprint had survived somewhat better, the masters and artists of Liège were brilliant exceptions to the prevailing mediocrity. Similarly in the French kingdom the only really active schools flourished in the regions which the

Carolingians had always regarded as conquered territories, to be exploited to the best advantage —in other words, in the South. All the centers of monarchical culture were concentrated in Neustria. In the year 1000 the best masters were at Reims (where the kings were crowned and anointed with oil from the Holy Ampulla)—in the monastery of Saint-Benoît-sur-Loire near Orléans, where the relics of St Benedict were preserved, where the panegyric of Robert the Pious was written and where, later, Philip I had himself buried—and, lastly, at Chartres. A century later the best teachers were still to be found at Chartres; also at Laon, Tournai, Angers, Orléans and Tours.

Outside these truly Frankish lands, traversed by the Rhine, the Meuse and the Seine, only two notable cultural developments call for mention. One of them, grafted on to the Neustrian branch, ramified little by little into the countries conquered by the Normans. First affected was Fécamp, next the Abbey of Bec, and before long Canterbury, York and Winchester followed suit—when in 1066 on both sides of the Channel a dynamic monarchy held sway and activated all the ferments that the Vikings had inseminated in this part of Europe in earlier times. Other, more venturesome developments were in progress in Catalonia where, in that furthest outpost of Christendom, bishops and abbots of the year 1000 welcomed the exotic skills coming from the Islamized lands. Such novelties as algebra, astronomy and the science of numbers particularly appealed to them. It was to Catalonia that the youthful Gerbert went to learn the technique of making astrolabes. This province, however, like Germany, had been entirely remolded by the Carolingians. Here the sense of the Arab peril, more instant and compulsive than elsewhere, kept alive the memory of Charlemagne, hero of the Islamic wars, precursor of the crusades, but also an enthusiastic patron of classical literature. So it was that in the cathedral of Vich, the abbeys of Ripoll, Cuxa and Montserrat, the masters kept to the traditional educational methods practised by Alcuin and Hrabanus Maurus, and enraptured their pupils with readings from the poets of Antiquity.

Poor masters, poor schools, and even poorer science—but at least true to their ideals and therefore capable, in a civilization that had sunk into almost complete barbarism, of keeping afloat an art pointing to better things. This much is clear: that the trickle of classical culture took its rise in royal palaces and the places of worship where the kings were anointed with the holy oil; and that the chroniclers who collated memories of their exploits treated the sovereigns as being at once men of God and avatars of Caesar. At first sight it may seem absurd that the flowers of classical rhetoric should have been lavished on mere tribal chiefs who tricked themselves out with strings of beads and dissipated their energies in futile forays. But these schools of learning, these libraries, these treasures whose finest cameos bore the profiles of Trajan and Tiberius, had anyhow the merit of ensuring, in a series of naive but fervent renaissances, the survival of a certain type of humanism. The roots of Suger's aesthetic, of the erudition of St Thomas Aquinas, of the whole Gothic efflorescence and the new creative freedom it engendered, were struck in these oases of culture that held their ground, undaunted, in a wilderness of semi-savagery.

But after 1000 the centers of classicism lost much of their lustre—coincidently with a decline in the personal power of the kings—and this change had a decisive effect on the evolution of art in the course of the eleventh century. By 980 these kings made their presence felt only in a limited part of their dominion and in the following decades their authority continued to dwindle throughout the western world, soonest and most rapidly in the kingdom of France. The sovereign lost nothing of his spiritual prestige, but prelates and provincial magnates ceased putting in an appearance at his court. In 1100 the only persons who attended its sessions were country squires living near Paris and some officers of the household. Feudality wound its way parasitically around the trunk of royalty; the throne was still its necessary prop, but little by little the overgrowth strangled the parent stem and soon the crown was no more than an ineffectual symbol. The real powers, the regalia, attributes of kingship—among them the upkeep of the churches, the task of decorating them, in short the control of art activities—were soon dispersed among a number of hands. In the second half of the eleventh century the greatest church-builder in northern France was no longer the king, but his vassal, the Duke of Normandy.

The authority of the German monarch did not disintegrate so rapidly; before 1140 the Germanic lands cannot be said to have become truly feudalized.

In Italy, however, the emperor was forced to recognize that the rights remaining to him were gradually passing from his hands. The main reason was that his personal power was being challenged by another, markedly in the ascendant: that of the Bishop of Rome. As early as the year 1000 Abbot William of Volpiano stressed this fact. "The might of the Roman Emperor to which heretofore all monarchs bowed throughout the world is wielded now in the various provinces by several sceptres; but the power of binding and loosing in heaven and on earth has been granted by an inviolable gift to the *magisterium* of St Peter." A hundred years later the Pope had gathered most of the Churches of the West under his sole sway, he boldly reprimanded kings and even in Germany made a bid to wrest his prerogatives from Caesar. Between 980 and 1140 two tendencies were strongly operative: one of them was the gradual collapse of monarchical authority in all the western lands, the other, more uniformly distributed throughout Latin Christendom, developed into a movement to reform the structure of the Church and, with this in view, to transfer *auctoritas* to the prelates, to bring them into close association with the Holy See and to limit the freedom of action claimed by the kings. These were the causes of the great divide in the evolution of western art that developed between the reigns of the Emperor Henry II and of St Louis of France: the break of continuity in the evolution of the major forms of art sponsored by royalty.

The reflux of the royal aesthetic synchronized with the decline in the institution of kingship. This movement began in that part of Europe in which from 980 on royalty was becoming, for all practical purposes, a dead letter: in the southern provinces. Here either the schools were languishing or the teaching in them was given a different orientation. Thus free scope was allowed to these distinctively "Romanizing" tendencies which had always been alive and active in the culture of the South of Europe.

For what was in process of emerging as a result of the ebbing of monarchical power in Provence, Aquitaine and Tuscany was in reality another visage of Rome. Not the one that had fascinated Charlemagne and still charmed Otto III and Abbon of Fleury: a visage whose features had been petrified as it were by recurrent phases of archaization and, for all their charm, now seemed elegant but "dead" as a line of Virgil. This other visage had nothing classical about it and took from Rome only those aspects which seemed viable in this new age of "modernity". Not that the classical tradition had ever died out; the Roman heritage survived in extant temples and amphitheatres and in certain cities where the ancient urban way of life still lingered on. It had stayed alive, but it had moved with the times, enriched itself with acquisitions from Byzantine Christendom, from the Coptic and Mozarabic cultures. The enfeeblement of royalty and the decline from favor of the cultural models artificially resuscitated by the emperors removed the obstacles to the flowering of new forms of art. In the eleventh century they sprang up from the ancient Latin roots; it was the same vigorous sap as that which engendered the triumph of the feudal system that brought them to fruition. The classical traditions of the monarchical schools were confronted by all that was not reverently buried in libraries and treasures, but answered to the needs of a living culture. Royal art, in fact, was ousted by Romanesque properly so called, the art that after the first millennium came triumphantly to flower in this new springtime of the western world.

II

FEUDALISM

THE THREE ORDERS

In the eyes of God—and in the eyes of his servants, the ninth-century churchmen—all men formed but a single people. They differed of course in race, sex, birth and social status. Yet, as Agobard, Archbishop of Lyons, had written in the time of Louis the Pious, "the one thing all insist on is a kingdom." Under the aegis of the king, in whom were vested both priestly and military functions, who both wielded temporal power and shouldered the collective responsibilities of the people towards the celestial principalities, all alike joined in an ordered progress towards the Light. Needless to say the people was divided; age-old barriers existed between laymen and churchmen, clerks and monks, and above all, in this age of serfdom, between freemen and those who were used like beasts of burden. Nevertheless, in the early Middle Ages, a small élite of high-ranking prelates, the only men capable of constructing an ideology, whose views alone are handed down to us by records of the period, pictured all God's children as "of a kind," and this notion of unity linked up with another leading idea, that of the stability of the social edifice and the monarchical institution. The Latin word *ordo* signified the immutability of the conditions of man's earthly existence. This "order" was imposed by God at the Creation; to every man He allotted his appointed place in a scheme of things that assigned him certain rights and specific duties in the gradual edification of the Kingdom of God. Anyone who tried to step outside the state to which God had called him did so at his peril; any act of this kind was sacrilege. On the day of his coronation the king gave a solemn pledge to accord to each of the social orders its due prerogatives. Thus the highly primitive world of the ninth century may well give an impression of having been impervious to change, determined for all time by the tempo of rural life in which the sequence of the seasons never varies and time moves in a cycle constant as that of the heavenly bodies. No one in that social system could nurse a hope of getting wealthy enough to improve his status and enter the higher grades of the temporal hierarchy. All the rich were heirs, owing their fortune and prestige to legacies handed down, generation after generation, from an immemorial past. And the poor were humble tillers of the soil that their ancestors had made fertile by the labors of their hands. Any change in their lot seemed accidental, any thought of it preposterous. God—like the kings, like the emperor —reigned supreme at the heart of things, sovereign of the immutable.

So it seemed; but actually the world was changing, if imperceptibly, and to a rhythm that was very gradually speeding up. As the year 1000 drew near and, to begin with, in the most highly evolved of the western provinces—the kingdom of France— new social structures were beginning to take form. The seeming "modernity" of the eleventh century comes from this new trend, so far-reaching as to affect all the aspects of civilization, most notably the manner in which power and wealth were distributed, the conception of man's relation to God and, as a result, the whole orientation of creative art. It is impossible to understand the emergence of the Romanesque and the forms it assumed without taking into account this change: the growth of what is known as the feudal system. The cause of this mutation was not economic; by and large the economy stagnated or progressed much too slowly to effect any considerable changes in the social structure. Its origin was rather of a political order, the steadily increasing impotency of the kings. Today the unity of power, when it lay in the hands of the great Carolingians, may well seem miraculous. How, one wonders, did these kings, little more than tribal chieftains, manage to keep under effective control a State so far-flung, so lacking in communications, so heterogeneous as was the Empire around 800? How did they succeed in reigning simultaneously over Friesland and Friuli, on the banks of the Elbe and at Barcelona; how was it that their word was law in townless, roadless territories where even the king's messengers had to travel on foot? Their authority was founded on a permanent state of war, an ever-extending range of conquests. Charlemagne's forbears had sallied forth from Austrasia at the head of a small troop of kinsmen, friends and faithful retainers who followed and obeyed them simply because they were victorious, shared out the booty of each campaign and were free to pillage to their hearts' content. The Carolingians had ensured the loyalty of these comrades of early days, their sons and nephews, by marriages, ties of kinship and those of vassalage. Every spring, when the grass began to grow and companies of mounted men could count on forage for their horses, they mustered all their friends, counts, bishops, abbots of the larger monasteries. Then there began the "open season" for forays, massacres, rape and rapine, with the king riding once again at the head of his troops towards the profitable thrills of some new campaign.

But already, as early as the ninth century, in the intervals between campaigns and in the autumn, when each of the sovereign's lieges was back on his ancestral domain, with his family, concubines, serfs, dependents, he was promptly freed from royal tutelage and, the roads being blocked, needed obey no law but his own. At these times the noble held unchallenged sway over all the cultivated lands around his castle and ruled despotically over a peasantry, aware indeed that a king existed but seeing him only as a shadowy figure, inaccessible and invisible as God Himself. For the countryfolk peace and prosperity depended entirely on the will of the local lord. In time of famine they could count on a dole of a few handfuls of wheat from his granaries and if he abused his powers, to whom could they complain? But soon after the revival of the Empire there came a moment when the kings ceased being war-makers; there were few if any military expeditions, no more lootings, no more spoils of war. Why then should the great of the land endure the hardships and perils of never-ending campaigns for the good pleasure of a ruler who had ceased to give them anything in return? Accordingly they spaced out their visits, fewer and fewer nobles attended the royal courts, and the State whose unity was based on periodical reunions of this kind gradually fell to pieces.

Its disintegration was speeded up by the Nordic, Saracen and Hungarian invasions. The Continent

and the off-shore islands were attacked by new enemies and fighting no longer took place outside the pale of Christendom but at its very heart. The effects of this were calamitous; heathen hordes swooped down on defenceless cities, burnt and looted, then retreated in boats or on horseback carrying off their plunder. Equipped for planned campaigns, slow to mobilize, the king's armies were quite incapable of forestalling these attacks and resisting them. In the constant onslaughts to which all Western Europe was exposed the only war leaders capable of restoring order were the petty princes of each region. They alone could muster all the able-bodied men at a moment's notice, maintain and equip a permanent force to garrison their strongposts, the castles, and the large fortified enclosures in which all the peasants of the region took refuge with their flocks and herds. It was to these local rulers, no longer to the ring, that the population looked for its defence. It was now that the power of royalty underwent a real decline. The notion of it lingered on in men's minds, but only as a legend having no contemporary validity, no bearing on everyday life or concrete reality. All prestige, all effective power, came to be vested in local chieftains, dukes and counts, hailed as the true heroes of the Christian Resistance. Armed with miraculous swords, helped by angelic hosts, they forced the invaders to turn tail, empty-handed. In the assemblies of warriors minstrels hymned in rousing strains the exploits of these gallant lords and openly derided the supineness of the sovereigns.

The West and South of Latin Christendom, regions which the Carolingians had never brought fully under control, and which had suffered most from inroads of marauders, were the starting point of parallel developments affecting the two chief sectors of society: the Church and the body of laymen. The men who had hitherto recruited the troops of each province under their banner, at the bidding of the king, their kinsman and their lord, broke completely with the sovereign. They still professed to be his loyal subjects and on occasion placed their joined hands between his, sign of homage; but they now treated as a heritage the judicial and executive powers which he had delegated to them. These they exploited freely and transmitted to their eldest sons. The greatest princes, the dukes, to whom fell the task of defending large areas of the kingdom, were the first to make good their autonomy (in the early tenth century). This political fragmentation did not make headway in the north and east of the former Carolingian empire; here the kings asserted their rights more vigorously and the age-old tribal institutions were more firmly rooted. But elsewhere it continued, and soon the counts, in turn, emancipated themselves from the dukes. Then, as the year 1000 approached, the principalities under the sway of counts followed suit and each of the barons who, in a region of forests and small cultivated tracts owned a stronghold, built up a little independent State around it. On the eve of the eleventh century new "kingdoms" were established everywhere, their rulers were crowned with all due pomp and ceremony, and no one called in question their status as God's lieutenants. Henceforth the central military and judicial power became more and more dispersed, broken up into an archipelago of isolated units, small and large.

Each had a master entitled "seigneur" or "sire" (equivalent to the Latin *dominus*, he who truly dominates). This title ("lord" in English) was the same as that assigned to "God" in Christian ceremonies. For the lord claimed the prerogatives of which, formerly, the king had the monopoly; his word was law. Like the sovereign he was well aware of belonging to a dynasty whose roots had been struck by his ancestors in the regions under his sway, and in the stronghold where he held assemblies of his vassals, and he also knew that his offspring would continue to draw sustenance from the same soil, century after century. In short the dynasty was a tree with a single stem, since like the royal crown the local lord's *auctoritas* was transmitted, indivisible, from father to son. Like the king, again, each lord felt it was his divinely imposed duty to maintain peace and justice in his domain, and the complex of rights enabling him to perform it converged on his castle. The tower, formerly a symbol of royal majesty under its military aspect, was now regarded as an affirmation both of personal power and of the prestige of a dynasty. "Men of noble birth and affluence," a chronicler of the early twelfth century tells us, "spend most of their time in warfare, on the battlefield; so as to guard himself against his enemies, to vanquish his equals and subjugate the weak, each makes a point of building the highest possible embankments and digging a broad, deep moat surrounding them. Crowning these fortifications is a rampart of squared treetrunks solidly nailed

together." Such was the castle of the period and though built on highly rustic lines, it served its purpose well, given the primitive nature of military skills. Secure behind his ramparts, the lord could snap his fingers at his rivals, even defy the king himself. The castle was the core, the vital center of political power and the new social structure that was emerging.

The changes in this structure reflected those that had recently taken place in the art of warfare. For it had become clear that the old-fashioned royal army, consisting of a mob of poorly equipped footsoldiers, was quite incapable of repelling the invaders of the ninth and tenth centuries. Only well-armed mounted troops protected by cuirasses could hold their ground, move promptly to threatened points and effectively pursue aggressors. So there was no longer any question of mobilizing the peasantry whose only weapons were staves and stones and who, in any case, lacked the spare time needed for training them in cavalry warfare. Thus military service was confined to a limited number of professional soldiers. The residents around the fortress, who fled to it for refuge in times of danger and therefore took orders directly from their lord, were by reason of the military specialization which had become indispensable divided into two well-defined classes, treated differently by their master, the owner of the castle. All alike were "his men," but the poor, the "yokels," who took no active share in the defence of his land, were treated by the lord as mere supernumeraries whom he protected but exploited without compunction. All these people belonged to him; they had ceased to be truly free, if no more slaves. All shared alike the burden of *corvées* and levies—the price they had to pay for the security assured them by the great landowner.

Unlike them, the few young men who still had the privilege of bearing arms enjoyed a real freedom. They escaped exploitation and oppression by the lord of the land since they took turns to garrison his castle; public safety had come to repose on the courage of this little band of mounted warriors, and they gallantly risked their lives defending it. Their duty towards the "master of the tower" was summed up in some honorable services deriving from the oath of vassalage and the homage they had paid to the owner of the castle. They were horsemen, "knights," and mustered as a squadron under the banner of the local lord, just as the large armies of eighth-century kings had enrolled under his banner for some foray. They formed in fact a replica, but on a smaller scale, of the royal court.

This new system of political and social obligations was an adjustment to the concrete realities over which the Carolingian sovereigns had temporarily triumphed, but which persisted beneath the surface in the social order of the day. Among the realities which had to be allowed for were the enterprise and energy of the aristocracy, the vastness of the great domains, too remote to be effectively controlled by the central power. The decentralization due to the feudal system was appropriate to a rural world split up into a host of hermetically sealed-off compartments. Master of all he surveyed, the lord of the castle cut the figure of a petty king, though he lacked an essential of kingship: he had not been consecrated. Hence a second development: the reaction of the Church to the new order.

The power of kings in the early Middle Ages had not trespassed on what, in this world, pertained to God: his sanctuaries and the rights of those appointed to His service. The sovereigns protected the Church and were careful not to exploit it too flagrantly. All the bishoprics and great monasteries were given charters whose terms forbade the levy of taxes by government officials on their domains and the requisitioning of their men. These privileges were imperilled by the disintegrating effect of feudalism and the increasing independence of the local authorities. Dukes, counts and lords of castles ensured the defence of the territory they controlled and claimed the right of judging, punishing and exploiting all its inhabitants (except the knights), even if they were representatives of the Church. This was a first infringement of the *status quo*. Moreover, being at a safe distance from the king and secure behind the walls of their castles, the strongest of these local lords usurped another royal prerogative; they claimed to be the guardians and patrons of the cathedrals and monasteries and, as such, to have the right of nominating bishops and abbots. Now, though the Church tolerated the selection of its dignitaries by the sovereign since he had been anointed and thus invested with spiritual power, it could not countenance high-handed conduct of this kind on the part of a duke, or count, who had only might, not right, on his side.

But in the conflict that ensued the Church lacked the backing of the king. The decline of royal executive power led the ecclesiastical authorities to claim for themselves the chief of the king's functions, that of maintaining peace. In former times God had delegated to the king, by the rite of coronation, powers that the sovereigns had now become incapable of exercising. Thus it was left to God to withdraw them from the king and to exercise them Himself, through the intermediary of His servants. The first claim to this right was voiced in southern Gaul, in Aquitaine and the county of Narbonne, a region in which, more keenly than elsewhere, the absence of a king had made itself felt. Solemn declarations of the overlordship of the Church were made in the late tenth century at great assemblies presided over by the bishops. Next, the idea made its way northwards by the valleys of the Rhone and the Saone and by 1030 had reached the northern frontiers of the kingdom of France. It did not cross them; beyond them lay the territory of the Emperor, still quite capable, unaided, of keeping peace and order in his dominions. But throughout France "the bishops, abbots and all those dedicated to our holy religion began to convene the people in Councils, to which were brought bodies of saints and countless shrines containing relics. Prelates and princes from all the land gathered together for the re-establishment of peace and the institution of our holy Faith. On a placard divided into chapters a list was drawn up of the acts that were prohibited and of the Christian's duties, accepted in the oath he swore to his Creator. Chief of them was the duty of maintaining an inviolable peace."

The Peace of God ensured special protection (like that formerly given by the kings) to the weakest, most vulnerable members of the community. God Himself ordained the immunity of places of worship and their precincts, of the churchmen and, lastly, of the poor. Any man who violated these sanctuaries and laid hands on the weak was to be anathematized and excluded from the community until he made due repentance. For he had incurred the wrath of God, invisible and dreadful Judge, who, unless He took mercy, would set loose on the offender all the powers of terror in this world and the next. "I will not force my way into a church in any manner since it is under God's protection; nor into the storerooms in the precinct of the church. I will not attack a monk or churchman if he be unarmed with earthly weapons, nor any of his company if he be without lance or buckler. I will not carry off his ox, cows, pig, sheep, goats, mare or unbroken colt, nor the faggot he is carrying. I will not lay hands on any peasant, man or woman, sergeant or merchant; nor take away their money or constrain them to pay ransom. I will not mistreat them by extorting their possessions on the ground that their lord is making war." These are among the vows solemnly enacted at one of the assemblies of the knights; to break them was tantamount to flinging oneself headfirst among the demons.

The first effect of this legislation was to mark out for reprobation a specific group of the community which, in the eyes of the Church, was constantly waging aggressive wars and responsible for the prevalent disorder of the age. A group that had to be guarded against and whose nefarious activities must be checked by ecclesiastical coercion, by inspiring it with terror of God's wrath. This class of men, treated as public enemies which, viewed from the angle of the naive dualism prevalent in the religious beliefs of this sadly unenlightened age, seemed an embodiment of the hosts of evil, was none other than the nobility, more exactly the body of mounted knights. It was the knights of his diocese whom Bishop Jordan of Limoges excommunicated, hurling anathemas at their weapons, even at their horses, instruments of their misdeeds, and at the insignia of their rank. Thus from now on the provisions of the Peace of God delimited more strictly still the warrior caste, which the waning of the king's authority and the redistribution of executive power were tending to isolate from the rest of the lay populace by assigning to it a specific function and certain privileges.

So it was that at the close of the tenth century the image of the social system was modified in the more cultivated circles of ecclesiastics. The notion of the division of the Christian community into categories or "orders" was still regarded as immutable. This was part of the scheme of things, established for all time. But henceforth it was posited that God had ordained the separation of mankind into three clearcut classes. "Human law recognizes but two classes; in practice the noble and the serf are not dominated by the same statutes. The nobles are warriors, defenders of churches, protectors of the people, great and small alike, themselves included.

The other class consists of serfs. But the city of God, commonly thought to be a single whole, has in reality three Orders: the men who pray, the men who fight and, thirdly, they who work. All three Orders coexist; none can dispense with the others; the services of each enable the others' tasks and each in turn assists the others." This passage in a political poem by Adalberon of Laon dedicated to King Robert of France is echoed in the remarks of another bishop, Gerard of Cambrai, of about the same date (c. 1030). "From its very origin the human race had been divided into three classes, all of which aid each other: the men who pray, the fighting men, the tillers of the soil." These latter were the enslaved mass of food-providers, "common folk," contrasting with the two élites, priests and warriors. Such was the notion of the social order which, inaugurated in the early eleventh century, was to be accepted throughout the western world for several centuries as a law of nature. It had at least the merit of putting an end to that involvement of the spiritual with the temporal, exemplified in the persona of the Carolingian kings, survivals of which can still be seen in the monarchies of around 1000. The break-through of the forces of feudalism put an end to this confusion, under their impact the veil fell from men's eyes and the basic cleavage between the spiritual and the temporal authorities became apparent. The feudal war-lords were not vested with religious functions or any other-worldly powers, while the churchmen took over all the charismatic missions hitherto reserved to royalty.

This point has its importance when we seek to trace the effect of the changed social conditions on the development of art. For in the course of the eleventh century the lay lords dispossessed the king to some extent of the resources he could freely draw on in the past; deprived of the emoluments enabling him to practise a luxurious way of life, he had less to spend on large-scale works of art. From now on any small surplus earned by manual workers passed almost entirely into the hands of the landed nobility, who spent much of it on their incessant wars and squandered what remained on elaborate festivities in which the leading knights indulged their taste for display. Nevertheless, even in the regions where the forces of political dissolution were most active and where the power of the monarchs was most drastically curbed—that is to say in southern Europe—money was still available to finance great works of art. For a slow but steady improvement in methods of agriculture, bringing larger crops, constantly increased the income of the feudal lords. Some part of it was diverted from worldly ostentation and devoted to a worthier purpose, the service of God, in which creative art participated. For the feudal nobility were God-fearing men and, as the kings had done, gave generous alms to the monks and clergy. So it was that the gifts of the high nobility replaced those of the monarchs; their pious donations provided the wherewithal for building, sculpture, painting. However, unlike the sovereigns, the feudal lords did not attempt to supervise and orient the activities of artists. They were not well-read men as the kings were (or aspired to be), nor like them did they have a personal liturgic function, for they had not been consecrated. Thus the aesthetic functions of royalty reverted to the Church, as did that other royal duty, the duty of maintaining public peace. But—and this was another outcome of the political and social upheaval—this ecclesiastical art took shape in a world crushed and brutalized by the dominance of the warrior caste. Hence the stamp it bears of an age of violence, of the culture of a class of men who, never having learnt to read or write, were incapable of reasoning and responsive only to gestures, rites and symbols: the culture of the knights.

THE POWERS OF EVIL

In the provinces south of the Loire and the Alps, where kingship was a dead letter and the Carolingians had failed solidly to establish the educational system reconstituted by Alcuin, eleventh-century artists did not employ the disciplined art language which reflected the teaching of the schools under the patronage of royalty. Put to the service of monasteries where to read the classics was regarded as a misguided, not to say pernicious hobby, and in which it was hoped to solve the mystery of things by mental processes as remote from reality as the stuff of dreams, art was identified with an exploration of the invisible. It was not concerned with representing what the eye sees; the data of visual experience were considered unworthy of serious interest, since the world of concrete things was imperfect and soon to pass away. The function of art was to figure forth the true reality concealed behind the veil of appearances, that ultimate reality of which the liturgical rites gave premonitory glimpses, pending its total revelation at the resurrection of the dead on the Last Day. The work of art was called on to lift the veil, and what it revealed to the beholder was not man, nor a God in the likeness of man, but the dark, secret forces which pervade and activate the cosmos.

Many of these forces were ambivalent. To eleventh-century man, even to a scholar who had pondered deeply on the Scriptures and the writings of the Fathers and thanks to them had cleared his mind of the gross superstitions of the people, it often seemed that the interventions of the unseen world in man's affairs were at once beneficent and maleficent. However, the progress in religious enlightenment was tending to dispel this ambiguity and to make it possible in speculations on the Other World to distinguish more surely between good and evil influences, light and darkness. Clearly the chief task of architect, sculptor, painter was to create visible counterparts of the powers of light, and so to build up an image of the Kingdom of God. But it was no less needful to represent the hostile forces lying in wait for man, laying traps for him, barring his path, forever seeking to lead him astray and hinder his progress to salvation. For the Christian soul must never relax its vigilance, it must be always on its guard, unsleeping, quick to detect the multifarious perils threatening it at every step. Committed as it was to a spiritual warfare, the whole monastic community had to be ever on the alert and the figurations of Evil were intended to remind the monks of the enemy at the gates.

In the symbolism of sin two "perverse" natures—that of woman, that of an animal, the serpent—are combined. In this age when so high a value was assigned to chastity, then regarded as the supreme virtue of the man of God, and extolled as one of the surest paths to salvation, there was a tendency to assimilate Eve to the serpent that tempted her. Though on the metopes of Modena cathedral she is still an innocent young woman and keeps at a safe distance the insidious reptile, at Autun it is otherwise; under the sculptor's chisel her body is beginning to acquire something of its sinuosity. And in the siren figures human and animal forms are frankly merged.

In the Garden of Eden there had been a pact, ordained by God, between man and the animals, who willingly submitted to his rule. This ended with the Fall; the beasts became a rebellious, dangerous mass of creatures, without speech or reason, sunk a degree deeper in the mire of brutish sensuality. It was admitted that domestic animals whose services were useful to man might have certain "virtues." As for creatures that crept and crawled, obviously they were Satan's allies. Even more sinister were the strange monsters described in medieval teratologies and seen in dreams. They were usually hybrids, half bird, half serpent, combining the forms of beasts of the air and beasts of the earth. Such was the basilisk, king of the creatures of the infernal regions, also the dragon of the Apocalypse, agent of chaos and destruction, against whom the archangels of the Lord—like the ancient heroes, founders of cities—would wage war on equal terms. Hell itself was given the look of a monster with huge gaping jaws. And it was in the guise of a raging beast that a painter represented the storm-tossed boat in which Jesus lay sleeping. This creature, with its horrific face, was an embodiment of the fears that haunted the minds of peasants huddled round their meagre fires in the dark night of the medieval world, or roving among the crowded charnel-houses where bodies of men and beasts, dead of hunger, lay rotting.

GIRL AND WINGED SNAKE. ABOUT 1130-1135. METOPE FROM MODENA CATHEDRAL.
MUSEO LAPIDARIO, MODENA CATHEDRAL.

GISLEBERTUS (ACTIVE FIRST THIRD OF THE 12TH CENTURY

THE TEMPTATION OF EVE. ABOUT 1120-1130. MUSÉE ROLIN, AUTUN.

PSALTER OF HENRY OF BLOIS: ANGEL LOCKING THE DAMNED IN HELL.
WINCHESTER, MID-12TH CENTURY. FOLIO 39, COTTON MS NERO C.IV, BRITISH MUSEUM, LONDON.

THE DESTRUCTION OF THE WORLD. ABOUT 1130. UPPER PART OF A SCULPTURED DOOR PILLAR.
ABBEY CHURCH OF SOUILLAC, PÉRIGORD.

BEATUS OF LIEBANA, COMMENTARIES ON THE APOCALYPSE: THE FLOOD. SAINT-SEVER, GASCONY, MID-11TH CENTURY.
FOLIO 85, MS LAT. 8878, BIBLIOTHÈQUE NATIONALE, PARIS.

GOSPEL BOOK OF HITDA OF MESCHEDE: CHRIST AND THE DISCIPLES IN THE STORM ON THE SEA OF GALILEE. ABOUT 1020.
FOLIO 117 RECTO, MS 1640, HESSISCHE LANDES- UND HOCHSCHULBIBLIOTHEK, DARMSTADT.

Hitherto he had not figured often in religious art. But he now acquired a prominent place in the Christian world-picture. Not, it is true, in the sector given a relative clarity by the educational centers; rather, in the vast domain then being taken over by the monastic rites and liturgy; a domain which, to strengthen its control over the masses, was welcoming popular superstitions that till now the clergy had tried their best to suppress. This involved the acceptance of much of the folklore relating to death: belief in the continued presence of the dead and apparitions of souls in Purgatory. Men were plunged into a nightworld full of the terrors that walk in darkness. Thus devils came to haunt the cloisters, to trouble the sleep of chaste and healthy men. To keep away these spectral presences, the Rule of Cluny enacted that lamps should be kept burning all night in the dormitory. But this did not prevent their "appearing by night at the hour when the bell is rung for Matins." Three times Rudolph Glaber saw the devil, the hideous being, his head ringed with a cone of leaping flames described in the Psychomachia and the Apocalypse. At the monastery of Saint-Léger, in the dim light of daybreak, he saw "rising up at the foot of his bed a sort of little man horrible to see, of low stature (it seemed), with a thin neck, haggard face, jet-black eyes, peaked, puckered brows, a narrow nose, a prominent mouth, blubber lips, a mean, receding chin, a goatee beard, hirsute, pointed ears, a shock of touseled hair, dog's teeth, a tapered skull, a bulging chest, a hump on his back, flapping buttocks, filthy clothes." At Saint-Bénigne in Dijon, then at Moûtiers, he was visited by "a very similar devil, probably the same one." Now Rudolph was far from being an ignoramus or particularly gullible. Which of the monks of Cluny had not had experience of these visitations from the underworld? Such encounters were of course exceptional. "We must not forget that when manifest prodigies meet the eyes of a man still in the flesh, whether the prodigies are the work of good or evil spirits, this man has not long to live on earth, after seeing such things."

How was one to know whence come these unearthly visitants? For Glaber the world of appearances and that of dreams still had the ambivalence with which the primitive mind invests them. In this respect the dualism latent in monastic thought

URNES (NORWAY), PORTAL OF THE STAVE CHURCH. 11TH CENTURY.

THE DESTRUCTION OF THE WORLD.
SCULPTURED PILLAR, PORTAL
OF THE ABBEY CHURCH, SOUILLAC. ABOUT 1130.

CAPITAL, CLOISTER OF SAN PEDRO DE GALLIGANS,
GERONA. 12TH CENTURY.

CAPITAL, CLOISTER OF SANTO DOMINGO DE SILOS,
NEAR BURGOS. 12TH CENTURY.

CAPITAL IN THE APSE OF TRINITY CHURCH
OR ABBAYE AUX DAMES (FOUNDED 1062), CAEN.

2

THE ENEMY

Eleventh-century Christianity was of its very nature Manichaean. These men, who hunted heretics and haled them to the stake so that the germs of corruption they disseminated should be consumed by fire, regarded the City of God as a beleaguered citadel in which the heavenly garrison withstood unsleepingly the onslaughts of the Satanic hosts. These latter did not fear the Lord, any more than the knights respected the interdicts of the Church, or wolves spared the peasants' sheep. In the provinces which had relapsed into anarchy, where there was no longer any central power capable of defending the populace against gangs of young swashbucklers who pillaged, burnt and destroyed for the sheer joy of destroying—how could the inhabitants fail to regard the world, indeed the universe, as split up in two parts, divided against itself? Anathemas and excommunications notwithstanding, the Peace of God had failed to establish itself on earth; nor, indeed, did it prevail in the world invisible. At the very foot of God's throne Michael and the devil joined combat, like champions in the tiltyard. No one supposed that at the end of time Good would wholly triumph over evil; all the Scriptures promised was a segregation: on the Judge's left yawned open for all eternity the bottomless pit of Evil.

God's almighty power was forever challenged by a determined adversary, Satan, the arch-enemy.

MAN-EATING DEVIL.
CAPITAL IN THE CHURCH
OF SAINT-PIERRE AT CHAUVIGNY,
POITOU. 12TH CENTURY.

ST GREGORY, MORALIA IN JOB:
FIGHT AGAINST THE DRAGON. CÎTEAUX, IIII.
FOLIO 4 VERSO, MS 168, BIBLIOTHÈQUE MUNICIPALE, DIJON.

THE TEMPTATION OF CHRIST. CAPITAL IN THE CHURCH OF SAINT-ANDOCHE
AT SAULIEU, BURGUNDY. 12TH CENTURY.

PROFANE MUSIC AND WOMAN. CAPITAL IN THE NAVE, CHURCH
OF THE MADELEINE AT VÉZELAY, BURGUNDY. ABOUT 1120-1150.

marked an advance, since it essayed to draw a clear-cut distinction between the good and evil powers.

For those who reflected seriously on the subject and tried to master their instinctive dread, Satan had not the seductive aspect he was to be given in the psychologically more advanced thirteenth century. He was for them a figure out of a nightmare, utterly devoid of charm, and there are curious resemblances between Glaber's vision of him and the wild creatures armed with claws on the capitals of Saint-Benoît-sur-Loire and Saulieu, half concealed by the tempting objects they are handling, almost all of them being women. To represent the Enemy artists employed two styles. One was linear, sinuous, directly stemming from certain barbarian images and characteristic, it seems, of the sea peoples of the northwest, Irish, English, Scandinavians. In these lands there was no Roman substratum and the Church had not been affected by the return to classicism promoted by the Carolingians. Christianity had crept into the indigenous culture-pattern without greatly disturbing it, adopted its stylistic formulas and mental figurations. On the portals of the stave churches of Norway, as in the illuminated manuscripts of Winchester, Satan had quite naturally found a place among the fantasies of Nordic folklore, with their overtones of magic and wizardry. Whereas in the cloisters of Catalonia, Castile and Rouergue, the image of Evil was adapted to the solid, well-knit forms of the fabled monsters of antiquity. The hunting scenes (conceived in a quite different spirit) which had adorned Late Roman sarcophagi were used to represent the struggles taking place in a human soul. We see centaurs and chimeras disporting themselves in a scrollwork of stylized flowers and foliage. But the artists in these provinces also sought to body forth less familiar beings, the bizarre winged creatures invented in the East which figured on the embroidered textiles used for wrapping relics. The man who carved the capitals at Chauvigny took inspiration from the Apocalypse when he made the image of the Great Whore, symbol of all erotic taboos. But it was on the deepest level of the collective psyche that he found the figure of the demon that feasts on human flesh, the werewolf. Using all the resources of plasticity, he offered to God a living image of man's terrors, so that by His grace He might dispel them.

THE KNIGHTS

Little by little in the eleventh century a term came into common use—in France to start with—as a synonym for a member of the aristocracy. In its Latin form "caballarius," it had designated merely a soldier who fought on horseback. But in the French-speaking lands the connotation of "chevalier" was narrowed down; it became equivalent to the English "knight." In French parlance the men who, mounted on their warhorses, lorded it over the common herd and terrorized even the monks, were referred to as "chevaliers." All these men had been formally initiated into the profession of arms. Some came from the old nobility many of whom were affiliated by family ties to the royal family during the early Middle Ages. Others were petty local lords, mere countryfolk just wealthy enough not to have to work with their hands and to maintain the equipment needed for active service in wartime. There were also members of a still poorer class, the henchmen whom the lords gathered round them in their castles, who slept near their masters in huge wooden halls and lived on their munificence; and, finally, a host of nondescript adventurers who voluntarily enrolled under a young leader, to fight under his standard, share with him the fortunes of war and join with him in bold, often remunerative forays. Medieval "chivalry," at first a body of men of very different origins, became a well-defined, united whole, thanks to its privileges, to its place at the apex of the political and social structure, and above all to the fact that all these men followed the same way of life, had the same hopes and qualifications—those of "specialists in warfare."

It was an essentially masculine society. The culture of the eleventh century shut its eyes to woman and gave her little or no place in its art. There are no effigies of female saints; only, on occasion, strange, shadowy figures with wasp-like eyes and a wandering gaze that disconcerts the observer. The few feminine figures with a certain charm that found their way into the imagery of the churches were the crowned Allegories, representing the months and the seasons, flotsam of the bygone classical aesthetic, with Latin verses in keeping with the theme appended—figures as unreal, as artificial as flowers of rhetoric. Very occasionally the Mother of God makes an appearance in group scenes from the Gospels, but she is a mere supernumerary, kept discreetly in the background, like the lord's wife in the assemblies of the warriors. Usually woman is given a sinuous, serpentine form like that of some malignant tare that has crept into the good wheat in order to taint it. For is she not lasciviousness incarnate, the germ of corruption denounced by preachers, Eve the temptress, responsible for the Fall and all the sins of the world?

The knighthood was not only purely masculine but a sodality of heirs, held together by bonds of kinship. The power of the living lord was founded on the prestige of his forbears, the wealth and renown bequeathed by them to the clan, a sacred trust that each generation transmitted to the next. When dukes, counts and lords replaced the kings and took over their prerogatives, they justified this by the fact that their lineage was linked up with the sovereign's in a tangled skein of kinships. "The titles of the nobility," wrote Bishop Adalberon, "come from the blood of the kings from whom they are descended." This is why the concept of ancestry played so large a part in the social system. Even the most bare-faced adventurer boasted of his blue blood, every knight was spurred to action by a cohort of the valiant dead who had brought glory to the family name and to whom he would have to render account in the Hereafter. Though the rank and file were for the most part forgotten, every noble knew the names of the great men of his House, for the jongleurs in their songs kept alive the memories of these eponymous heroes. Thus they won a place in the annals of the race, and an undying fame. Their bodies lay side by side in the family vault built in ancient times by the founder of the lineage, and the chief religious rites centered on these tombs. Indeed, the Christianity of the year 1000, conditioned as it was by the mores of the aristocracy, gives an impression of being concerned primarily with a cult of the dead. This strong family feeling shared by the members of a line, which led them to hasten to the rescue when one of the clan was attacked and, if he fell, to join in taking vengeance on the relatives of the aggressor, may have persuaded the Church authorities to endorse the view that after a man's death living members of the family could help him on the path of salvation and purchase indulgences on his behalf. Almost all the alms given by the knights, who more than any others provided the wherewithal for artistic creation, were intended to ensure the well-being of dead members of the line in the after-world.

In this social order it was the so-called "young" who set the tone. Actually they were men in the prime of life, who had undergone their training and made proof of skill and valor in the public ceremony of initiation whereby they qualified as full-fledged members of the knighthood. None the less for a long while yet—so long as the young knight's father lived and he had not yet received from his hands the management of the estate—he chafed at the feeling of dependence, inevitable in a purely agrarian economy, so long as he stayed at home. So he left home at the earliest opportunity, roved the world with friends of his own age, in quest of pleasure, plunder and adventure. Hence the qualities most valued in the "perfect knight" were courage, physical strength, pugnacity. The hero whom all wished to emulate, whose exploits were recounted in the vulgar tongue at the gatherings of warriors, was an athlete of the stature suitable for combat on horseback: stalwart, thick-set, steady as a rock. Only the body counted, the heart as well, but not the mind. For the embryo knight did not learn to read, study might cramp his mettle, the knight was, purposely, illiterate. His proper sphere was warfare, real or mimic —the only activity that seemed worth while, that gave existence its savor, the great game in which a man stakes all, his honor and his life, but from which, also, those who succeed come home rich, triumphant, haloed with a glory worthy of their forbears, a fame whose echoes will go on resounding through the ages. The culture of eleventh-century Europe, shaped so largely by the warriors, was almost wholly based on a thirst for conquest, rapine, feats of derring-do.

But fighting took place only in fine weather and the "virtues" of the knight were not solely of a military order. Caught up in the elaborate network of loyalties and moral obligations which, when the king's power had ceased to function, enforced at least a semblance of discipline on the Western aristocracy, the chivalric hero was at once a lord and a vassal. He had to prove himself as generous as the best of lords, loyal as the best of vassals. Like the king, lord of lords, his model, the good knight was expected to be open-handed; *noblesse oblige,* and he felt bound to distribute all he had to those he cherished. After discarding his entire estate piecemeal, giving it to his "men," a Duke of Normandy announced: "I shall make over to you all my chattels: brassards, swordbelts, breastplates, helmets, leggings, horses, battleaxes and these fine, richly adorned swords. Always when dwelling in my house shall you enjoy my benefactions and the glory won by chivalrous exploits if you devote yourself with a good heart to my service." First, then, came largesse, cardinal virtue on a par with loyalty. No man could hold his head up in gatherings of the warriors if ever he broke the fealty he had sworn to. At this level of the social order the solidarity of the community hinged on a system of personal and collective oaths and on the mutual obligations they entailed. Boldness, energy, generosity, fidelity—these were the facets of that master value "honor," forever at stake on the battlefield and in the rivalries of the feudal courts.

Some familiarity with these conventions and the mental attitudes from which they sprang is needed for an understanding of the specific qualities and directives of the works of art produced during this period. Needless to say they were not made under the orders of the warriors, nor for their own use. True, these men had a passion for personal adornment; the hilts of their swords were made by skilled artisans; their wives and daughters richly embroidered the garments they wore on State occasions and the fabrics draping their great halls and the walls of seignorial chapels. But, flimsy or fragile for the most part, these things were by-products, mere excrescences of the domain in which architecture, sculpture and painting reigned supreme. In those days the work of art *par excellence* was a church; the one great art was sacred art. As in the past, it was the king and the churchmen who supervised and tended it, to the exclusion of all others. Yet—and this was something new—the spirit of chivalry was gradually invading this domain, and striking deep. Now that their power was faltering under the onslaughts of feudalism, the kings of France and England and soon the emperor himself came more and more to have a feeling that they, too, were becoming knights. How, indeed, draw any clear distinction between their status and that of a private *seigneur*? The ethic of the warrior caste was coming to impose its standards on their way of life. As for the Church, it was now under the rule of laymen—meaning, here too, the knights.

For every church was situated at the center of a seigniorial domain which provided the priests-in-charge with their sustenance. Like any feudal baron, every bishop, every abbot, every canon "owned" a host of peasants over whom he exercised judicial powers. When he held sessions, he was surrounded by vassals, he built towers, and when he entered the cloister was attended by a bodyguard of turbulent retainers, fighting men. Knights came and knelt, bare-headed, before him, placed their hands between his to signify they were "his men," and after swearing on the sacred relics to keep fealty were invested with a fief. These servants of God were also "bonny fighters." Was it not their duty to defend the property of their patron saints against aggressors and to risk their lives in campaigns for the enlargement of their Master's kingdom? When a bishop came to visit the Cid, El Campeador, he said: "Today I said Mass on your behalf; I have left my land and come to join you, for I desire to kill some Moors. I wish to do honor to my rank and, so as to deal more doughty blows, to be posted in the forefront of the fray." When they sallied forth, helmeted, at the head of a band of young prelates attached to their church, the virtues of honor, loyalty and courage meant as much to them as to the knights, their rivals. Though they knew it their duty to maintain the Peace of God, this did not mean they had to refrain from warfare; on the contrary, the Pax Dei had to be won by the sword —it was an aftermath of victory. As for the spirit of poverty, there was no trace of it in the Church of the year 1000. Given an assured place in the feudal system and by reason of their wealth and eminence ranking beside royalty (and indeed aspiring to dominate it, the more the prestige of the throne declined), the high ecclesiastical dignitaries took for granted that God desired the Church to wield temporal power and that wealth was a necessary

mainstay of its domination. When the churchmen inveighed against the knights and called them Satan's henchmen, this was often because they saw in them rivals of their own seigniorial power, dangerous competitors whose activities might lessen the profits made by exploiting the workers. Characteristic of the Church of this period was a will to power, coupled with a taste for fighting.

All great prelates and most of the monks came of noble families. So long as the right of nominating bishops and abbots rested with the king he kept to the practice of his Carolingian predecessors and chose persons of high birth. In a society whose structure was so rigorously determined by ties of blood, all the virtues—above all, perhaps, a gift for leadership—could stem from one source only, a man's ancestry. To assign the highest posts in the Church, those that gave the holders wide authority, to other than high-born men would have seemed like flouting the divine plan of reserving governance, and all seigniorial powers, to a certain breed of men. As for the feudal lords, when they had succeeded in wresting from the sovereign the patronage of a church, they regarded and treated it as a personal asset and exploited it like any other part of their belongings. Sometimes they kept to themselves the titular right of an abbacy and gave it to one of their sons or to some vassal as a reward for faithful service. And exactly the same rite as that of feudal investiture, the transfer of a symbolic object from the patron's hand to the beneficiary's, was employed by the emperor, by kings and barons for the granting of high posts in the Church. Ritual gestures of this kind had so much importance that ecclesiastical benefices came to be commonly viewed as fiefs constraining their holders to service and transforming them into vassals. Thus the Church became more and more tied up with the feudal system, the intrusion of temporal into spiritual affairs ever more pronounced. The services of the lay lord tended to take precedence over the service of God, priests to become less and less distinguishable from laymen. How, indeed, could this have been prevented? Knights, their brothers and cousins, forgathered with the canons and these latter no longer led the coenobitic life prescribed by the ancient Rules. They administered like other lords the estates which were their prebends; they hunted, rode the best horses, wore fine accoutrement, and many lived with women. Their only signal difference from laymen was the result of a special type of education and a veneer of scholarly culture, possessed by all high-ranking ecclesiastics and disdained by the knights. But even this veneer was disappearing. Under the feudal prelates the schools stagnated and in the diminution of the educational facilities provided by the Carolingians in monasteries and cathedrals, along with the progressive decline of humanistic values that can be traced in all the works of art produced in the eleventh century, we see one and not the least striking of the effects of the intrusion of the knightly spirit into the mores of the clergy.

It had an even deeper influence on the structure of religious thought and, as a result, on the trends of sacred art. Mixing freely as they did with members of the feudal courts, in which the nobles flaunted their social superiority by luxurious living, squandering and ostentation, clerics and monks gradually came to adopt their standards, to set store on gaudy ornaments, on objects that sparkled, made of the costliest gems and metals. Like the feudal princes and with a similar purpose—to prove her eminence in the hierarchy of powers ordained by the Will of God—the Church of the eleventh century decked herself with gold and jewels. She convinced the nobility of their duty to contribute some of their wealth to the service of God, and to set forth around the altars and, before dying, to hang around the necks of the reliquary "idols" the goldware and gems they had amassed in their forays. The kings set the example. To Cluny Henry II of Germany bequeathed "his golden sceptre, his golden globe, his imperial golden vestment, his golden crown and crucifix, weighing in all one hundred pounds." The monk at Saint-Benoît-sur-Loire who wrote the biography of King Robert describes in detail all the valuable objects that the churches at Orléans had been given by the king, stating their weight and value: in one case sixty pounds of silver, in another one hundred sols of gold, also an onyx vase bought for sixty livres. "He had the table of St Peter to whom the church is dedicated entirely covered with fine gold; after the death of the very holy king, Queen Constance, his widow, had seven livres of this gold withdrawn from the table and gave it to God and St Aignan for the embellishment of the roof of the convent she had built." All the nobles, according to their means, emulated the king's largesse. The Duke of Aquitaine presented the church of Saint-Cybard at Angoulême with "a cross of gold adorned with

precious stones weighing seven pounds, and some silver candelabra weighing fifteen pounds, wrought by Saracens." This last item evidently formed part of the loot, after some combat with a Moslem host on the frontiers of Christendom. "The booty they took came to an enormous weight of metal; for it is a custom of the Saracens to deck themselves for the fray with plaques of gold and silver. Mindful of the vow they had sworn to God, the knights made haste to send all this gold and silver to the monastery of Cluny, and with it the Abbot, St Odilo, made a most beauteous ciborium for the altar of St Peter." All the glittering jewelry that pagan kings in former times had caused to be buried with them in their tombs was now accumulated in the House of God, making it more resplendent than the thrones of the greatest princes of the earth. In the midst of a half-starved peasantry the knights squandered their resources light-heartedly, but the Church guarded its wealth in order to enhance the splendor of its rites and make them even more sumptuous and spectacular than the great feudal fêtes. For was it not fitting that God should manifest Himself in the most gorgeous of "glories," surrounded by that blaze of light ineffable which the sculptors of the Romanesque apocalypses figured forth symbolically as an almond-shaped nimbus enveloping His body? Was He not entitled to own a treasure more magnificent than that of all the great ones of the earth?

For He is God the Lord. The image of His authority all men conjured up was in the spirit of the age: feudal through and through. When he described the Almighty enthroned in the world invisible, St Anselm placed Him at the summit of a hierarchy of personal dependencies; the angels held fiefs granted by Him and behaved as His vassals —His "thegns," as the Old-English poet Cynewulf called them. All the monks pictured themselves as fighting for Him on much the same terms as the domestic warriors, the lord's "men," who as of right counted on a reward for their loyal service; on recovering, for example, a lost heritage, or a tenure confiscated in days gone by as a punishment for some misdeed of their forbears. As for the ordinary layman, the church relegated him, in respect of divine grace, to the abject condition of the enslaved peasant. Bishop Eberhart went so far as to describe Christ as his Father's vassal. The subjection of mankind to the Lord God was assimilated to the relationship between the vassals as a body and their feudal lord. The Christian promised fealty and service to his God; thus it was that the posture of the vassal doing homage, bending his knee to his lord, bare-headed, his hands clasped, became in this period the attitude of Christian prayer. But just as the contract of vassalage engaged both parties to aid each other, just as the feudal lord was obliged to succor "his man," provided the latter carried out his duties, just as the owners of great domains felt obliged in time of famine to distribute food to their peasants and, lastly, just as generosity was regarded as the cardinal virtue of the man of property, so the Christian, vassal of his God, looked to receive from Him protection from the dangers of this world and, crowning all, that eternal fief—his meed of paradise.

The lords' best gifts went to the bravest warriors, as rewards for valiant exploits. And it was by his exploits that a man hoped to win God's especial favor. This cult of knightly values gave eleventh-century Christianity an heroic cast; the greatest saints of the time were fighters. Like St Alexis, one of whose poems (datable to about 1040), composed in the vernacular for a princely court in Normandy, glorifies the feats of asceticism, these heroes of the faith were paragons of chivalry, muscular young Christians who dedicated to their Lord's service not only their stamina but also their physical sufferings. It must have been an effort for a community whose standards were set by a group of swashbuckling horsemen to hearken to the Gospel message of humility, compassion, loving-kindness. So, in order to appeal to a congregation of young knights and bring them back to God, the priests (who like them had grown up in the shadow of the lord's castle and like them were his servitors) stressed the idea of a Church Militant, led to the fray by Jesus brandishing banner-wise the Cross. They dilated on the lives of warrior saints like Maurice and Demetrius, urging their hearers to display an equal courage in their fight with that invisible but formidable foe, Satan's army. Such was the hold of the idea of chivalry that even mental activities were pictured as a sort of combat. Did not even the heavenly bodies battle with each other? Had not the monk Adémar de Chabannes seen one night "two stars in the sign of the Lion jousting with each other, the small one rushing at the big one, furious but fearful, and the big one hustling it with its mane of rays towards the west"? Christians faced up to the mysterious forces of the universe as they faced the enemy in feudal warfare. Virtue entailed constant watchfulness, a series of pitched battles with treacherous assailants. Every man pictured his individual life as a beleaguered tower which he was in honor bound to defend and hand back intact to his Lord. At the Last Day his courage and his failings would be weighed in the scales. Some Romanesque frescoes show us a warlike Christ gripping between clenched teeth the sword of justice and of victory.

The vocation of the knight was in a sense equivocal. The weapons God placed in his hands—those long swords which in the legends are always miraculous, sometimes inset with relics so as to enhance their magic power, and to which during the eleventh century a priestly benediction was often given—were used by the knight for the defence of the people. In this duty he had divine assistance, for the knighthood was the bulwark of Christendom against the pagan hordes. In practice, however, he often wielded his sword for selfish ends, to gratify his predatory instincts. And by so doing he enlisted in the hosts of evil.

The monks of the West saw in the knight an embodiment of evil; militia, malicia—*did not the very tongue in which God expressed himself, classical Latin, point to an equivalence between maleficence and knighthood? Such ambivalences—not to say contradictions—in the functions of a social group were tokens of the cleavage in the created world, in which the heavenly hosts waged endless combat with the emissaries of Satan. The tower, symbol of peace and of the mission of protection that, now the king was powerless, had passed into the hands of the warrior class, had also come to seem a symbol of armed aggression, of the violence and rapine in which the aristocracy delighted. A place of refuge to which the countryfolk could resort in time of trouble, the castle was also a lair from which troops of mounted men poured forth from time to time to rob the common people of their meagre gains. The foursquare castle tower had the same structure as the heavenly Jerusalem, citadel of just men made perfect. But when the painter of the Saint-Sever* Apocalypse *encircles it with the baneful Serpent, it evokes Babylon, corruption, city of Evil, at once alluring and alarming.*

Eleventh-century chivalry did not create; it destroyed. What of its culture has survived? A mere handful of charming songs, some of which, after 1100, seemed worthy of being committed to writing. Almost all the castles were built of wood and no trace of them remains except the mounds on which they stood. However, soon after the year 1000, the feudal lords of Anjou, influenced no doubt by the current vogue for rebuilding churches, took to replacing the wooden towers with large stone edifices. Between these fortresses and the towers built on the fronts of Norman abbeys, there was a marked family likeness, due no doubt to the association in religious symbolism of scenes of combat with the image of God triumphant over the powers of Evil. It was for the adornment of a cathedral (at Bayeux) that about 1095 Norman princesses embroidered on a band of linen, 231 feet long, a design in the Scandinavian manner representing episodes of the conquest of England. Had not Duke William crossed the sea as a soldier of Christ to punish a perjurer and to amend the evil ways of the English church?

SCENES FROM THE BAYEUX TAPESTRY. ABOUT 1095. MUSÉE DE LA REINE MATHILDE, BAYEUX.

THE CASTLE TOWER AT LOCHES (INDRE-ET-LOIRE). 11TH CENTURY.

THE TOWER OF LONDON: INTERIOR OF THE NORMAN CHAPEL OF ST JOHN IN THE WHITE TOWER. AFTER 1078.

BEATUS OF LIEBANA, COMMENTARIES ON THE APOCALYPSE: BABYLON. SAINT-SEVER, GASCONY, MID-11TH CENTURY.
FOLIO 217, MS LAT. 8878, BIBLIOTHÈQUE NATIONALE, PARIS.

90

SALVATION

God the Lord, this terrible God wielding a sword —how was one to render Him the services He required, how win His favor? Was it a matter of obeying His laws? But what were those laws? There can be no knowing what glimpses of the Gospel message were imparted to the peasants massed at the portal of the church when services were being held, who had to watch the priest's gestures from a distance, and heard snatches of hymns which, sung in Latin, were incomprehensible to them. What could these simple folk get from a clergy recruited among the serfs of the domain, from the village priest who, in order to support a wife and children, had to push the plough himself and soon forgot what little he had learned at school? One wonders how these priests themselves pictured the Saviour and what they really understood of His teaching. Hardly more is known of the religion of the knights, except that for them it was essentially a matter of rites, gestures, mechanical responses—to the exclusion of all else. For reading and writing had no place in their culture; theirs was a religion based on spoken words and images, that is to say on formalism. When a warrior came to take his oath what really counted, to his thinking, was not the dedication of his soul but the touch of his hand on a holy object: the cross on which he placed it, the Bible, or a bag of sacred relics. When he stepped forward to become his lord's "man," it was once again an attitude that counted, a special position of his hands, a string of words prescribed by use and wont, and the mere fact of uttering them sealed the compact with his lord. Likewise, on entering into possession of a fief he made a significant gesture, took in his hand a symbolic object. Submerged by the dark powers of nature, trembling at the thought of death and all that followed it, the knight clung to rites, his only safeguard. For they, he felt assured, would win God's mercy. He might solemnly confess his sins, but what saved him was a cultic gesture: his act of homage when he proffered to God his right-hand glove, symbol of fealty that the archangel Gabriel,

coming from heaven, would carry aloft to the Ruler of the Universe. The highest eulogy King Robert the Pious was given by his biographer was for the exceptional care he gave to ceremonies, "ordering them so minutely that in them God did not seem to be greeted by another's pomp but to be hallowed with the very glory of His own majesty." During his long death-agony this king, following the monks' example, sang psalms unceasingly and when his last moment came "he made again and again the sign of the cross on his eyelids, lips, neck and ears."

Basic to all these rites, physical counterparts of mental images, was a certain conception of God. This was twofold, as was the concept all men had first of the king, then of the feudal lord, when he took over the monarchic attributes. Arbiter of war and peace, he wielded both the sword and the sceptre. The eleventh-century God differed but little from the war-lords who laid ambushes in the marshlands to trap and wipe out the last Nordic pillagers in the year 1000. Every man was called on to join His army and share in the attack on those malignant powers which make their presence known from time to time in premonitory visions of death, by eerie rustlings after nightfall, but which—as was common knowledge—were the rulers of a world behind the world, of which men saw but the outer husk. These hidden powers were held to be infallible and invincible; hence the belief in judgment by ordeal. If two men were suspected of a crime the culprit could be distinguished from the innocent man by applying a piece of red-hot iron to both, and the nature of the scars would reveal which was guilty. Or else they could be thrown bound into water, which receives the innocent and rejects the guilty. None questioned the magical powers of the elements and in such ordeals their verdict was final. For sometimes in God's war with sin, whose issue the Christian could not help regarding as precarious, difficult cases arose, in which the All Highest had need of men to aid Him.

None the less, for the eleventh-century Christian the power of God was manifested most clearly in acts of justice, just as the power of the owner of his tenement was for the peasant, and that of the master of his fief was for the knight. God was He who punished; the most familiar image of Him was the majestic figure posted by Romanesque sculptors of the late eleventh century at the gates of monasteries, showing Him on the judgment seat, attended by His vassals. These "barons" His assessors were not as yet the Apostles, but the Elders of the Apocalypse and the Archangels, *duces* of the heavenly hosts. One of them, St Michael, took his stand in front of the throne, like a seneschal; his function was to keep order and perform the duties of a "clerk of the court." For God administered justice in the same manner as the feudal lords. The accused man, when he appeared before one of the many assemblies convened to reconcile knights and settle disputes between warring clans, was never alone. He was supported by friends who swore to his innocence and he could count on seeing among the members of the court men who were bound to him by family ties or reciprocal vows of fealty and would speak up for him, perhaps sway the verdict in his favor. This is why, dreading the prospect of the Last Judgment, so many of the men of this age were at such pains to earn the good will of the saints. These heroes of the faith composed God's tribunal, it would give ear to their pleadings, they would allay the divine wrath. So it was possible for everyone to make sure of an intercessor, to enlist "a friend in court" by the same method as that which made a good impression on an earthly court: by gifts. "Make to yourselves friends [in heaven] with the mammon of unrighteousness": this precept often figures in the records placed in the storerooms of monasteries, listing offerings made by the nobility. Saints existed everywhere; though their true abode was the unseen world, one might get in touch with them on earth, in certain places, for instance in churches dedicated to them, some of which housed their mortal remains. Through the intermediary of the priests officiating in these churches the saints could receive alms, the gifts which, it was assumed, would dispose them favorably to the giver. It was by generous donations distributed among a number of religious foundations that the eleventh-century knight, unable to curb his appetite for violence, even to discern what the Master expected of him, but haunted by a sense of guilt and a dread, whatever amends he made and however contrite he might be, of punishment, took steps to become a *persona grata* with the celestial court before which he must one day come to trial.

In the practices of terrestrial justice giving also served a purpose—to regain the favor of the lord. The feudal courts very rarely inflicted corporal punishments and the sentence usually took the form of a money payment. The object was to restore the social tranquillity that had been ruptured by the offender and to do away with a desire for revenge on the part not only of the injured party but also of his kinsmen and of the lord responsible for public order. For he regarded the conduct of the man who by an act of violence had broken the peace whose guardian he was as a personal affront. Therefore the guilty party was condemned to pay a fine in addition to a monetary compensation awarded to the family of the victim. This fine was to make amends for the damage that the king, the count or the lord of the castle—all responsible for public order—had suffered as a result of the crime committed. In the same way God's pardon could be bought. "Alms wash away sin as water extinguishes fire" was a dictum that often recurred in cartularies. A donation to God was by common consent the fundamental act of piety in this highly primitive Christendom still laboring under a sense of ineradicable guilt.

Giving to God did not mean giving to the poor. Who indeed but the lord did not cut the figure of a pauper, given the scanty yield wrung from the soil? Poverty was the common lot; its only remedies lay in the normal functioning of the seignorial institutions and the generosity natural to the men of high estate. True, Robert the Pious kept open house to the poor. On Maundy Thursday "kneeling on the ground, he delivered with his holy hands into the hands of each of them fish, vegetables, bread and a penny"; twelve of them always accompanied him on his travels and "to replace the ones who died he always kept a large reserve, so that their number never declined." But the symbolic side of these acts of charity must not be overlooked; they were not prompted only by compassion, but were also a ritual evocation of the Gospel narrative. The twelve men who accompanied the king played the part of the twelve Apostles, the distribution of food was a recall of the Last Supper. In practice all the donations made to appease God's wrath went to the churches.

It was to them that the men and women who had not won a place in the closed ranks of God's servants and were exposed to the onslaughts of Satan and his host offered their most precious possessions. Some even gave their persons and their offspring; hence the increase (especially within the Empire) of the host of "servants of the altar" as they were called, those who every year at the festival of the church's patron saint, whose "man" they had become, lined up in Indian file to lay on the stone of sacrifice the symbolic penny, token of their voluntary servitude. But everyone without exception was called on to donate a moiety of his worldly goods, his jewels and, more frequently, his land, the only real form of wealth. Donations were given whenever expiation had to be made for a specific sin, but it was above all on a man's deathbed that alms were most needed and most salutary.

The representations of the pains of hell that, following the revival of monumental sculpture, were systematically placed on the forefront of Cluniac basilicas in the last decades of the eleventh century were the end-product of a form of propaganda, some elements of which had made their first appearance around 1040. Striking fear into the hearts of all beholders, they led to a further increase in the number of donations *in articulo mortis*. These gifts did not merely serve the turn of the man who made them; he had in mind not only his personal salvation but that of the members of his family. When he divested himself of his property and drew on the wealth bequeathed by his ancestors, it was as much to benefit the souls of his dead forbears as for his own salvation. And he hoped on the Day of Judgment to pass as it were unnoticed in the midst of that undying entity, the race, which shouldered, collectively, the responsibility of each individual. This steady flow of pious gifts certainly did much to stimulate what was in effect the most active economic movement of an age only just emerging from complete stagnation. It implemented the only considerable transfers of wealth that took place, those arising out of successional partitions. These gifts impoverished the lay aristocracy and enriched the Church. They largely outweighed the extortions of the knights, at whose expense they enlarged the resources of the ecclesiastical power. But for the huge influx of new property and money, added year by year to the patrimony of the saints and providing their servitors with steadily increasing funds, there

could hardly have developed that creative urge which between 980 and 1140 gave rise to such remarkable achievements in European art. The flowering of Romanesque was nourished by the gradual progress of agriculture, but there would never have been this amazing spurt of energy had not the knighthood so gladly dedicated to God so large a portion of its wealth.

There was another means of making oneself acceptable to God and to His powers and principalities, another way of stripping oneself of worldly goods, but it asked more of one's body and one's soul—and this was a pilgrimage. What better offering could a man make to God and to the saints whose tombs he proposed to visit than the act of quitting his family and the safety of his home and launching out into the sea of troubles awaiting the medieval traveler once he had crossed his threshold? Pilgrimage was the most effective form of asceticism which eleventh-century Christianity, imbued with the heroic ideal, proposed to the knight concerned for his soul's salvation. It was an act of penitence which bishops habitually enjoined as a means of purifying the soul. It was also a symbol; in his wayfaring the pilgrim felt he was imitating the long, slow journey of the chosen people to the Promised Land and wending his way to the heavenly Jerusalem. And, lastly, pilgrimage was a pleasure; traveling, especially in the company of friends (as was usually the case), was the most enjoyable experience one could hope for. While they made their way on foot or horseback along forest tracks or sailed up the rivers, these bands of dedicated travelers differed little from the bands of young knights errant riding out in quest of adventure, and even less from the troops of vassals who, at the bidding of their lord, went to attend sessions of his court. For the pilgrims, too, were performing an aulic duty, that of gathering on an appointed day to pay homage to the saintly bodies enshrined in golden reliquaries studded with gems. Unseen forces emanated from these sacred objects, they healed bodies, ministered to troubled souls. And all were convinced that the mysterious beings whose mortal remains lay in these reliquaries would bestow their help and loving-kindness on those who had come so far to pay their respects to them. Such books as *The Miracles of St Foy* and *The Miracles of St Benedict* furnished lists, compiled by monks, of miraculous cures proving the efficacity of these pilgrimages.

The pilgrims usually made their devotional journeys in successive stages, with a halt at each of the shrines containing relics. Wishing to prepare for death King Robert with his court set out in Lent to pay his respects to all the saints "conjoined with him in the service of God." His long wayfaring took him to Bourges, Souvigny, Brioude, Saint-Gille-du-Gard, Castres, Toulouse, Sainte-Foy-de-Conques and Saint-Géraud-d'Aurillac. It is interesting to observe that he followed exactly the same route as anyone interested in Romanesque art today would choose. For during the eleventh century, and particularly in the southern provinces where the king's power was declining, the most advanced architecture was to be found in the vicinity of the miracle-working tombs. Here it was that the creative imagination which engendered the boldest inventions and innovations of monumental sculpture was given fullest scope. This upsurge of creativity was largely due to the vast sums of money donated by the crowds of pilgrims flocking to the shrines. Here, for example, is an account of one of the treasures then drawn on for the decoration of altars and the renovation of religious edifices. "What above all contributed to its increase was the tomb of St Trond where every day new and wondrous miracles took place. Such was its fame that for a good half mile around the little town all roads leading to the tomb and even fields and meadows were daily crowded with pilgrims of all classes, ranging from the nobility to the humblest peasants, above all on feast-days. Those who, because of the great press, could not find lodgings made shift to dwell in tents or shelters hastily put together with branches and curtains. One would have thought that they had gathered round the town to lay siege to it. They were attended by a whole host of merchants whose horses, carriages, carts and beasts of burden were kept busy all day supplying the pilgrims with food. Words fail to enumerate the offerings placed on the altar. Nor can we give an account of all the beasts, horses, oxen, cows, pigs, sheep and ewes brought thither, in number like the sands of the sea. Nor can we assess the quantity and value of the fine linen, wax, bread and cheeses. To gather in all the silverware and the pieces of money which poured in without cease until nightfall several sacristans had to labor without a moment's respite."

In the eleventh century the most cherished dream of every fervent Christian who hoped to win the divine mercy by a pilgrimage was that some day it would be given him to pray at the three most famous tombs: of St Peter, St James and Christ Himself. William, Duke of Aquitaine, "had formed a habit in his youth of going to Rome, seat of the apostles, every year and if perchance he could not do so made up for it by a devotional journey to St James's tomb in Galicia." Shortly before his death (in October 1026) the Count of Angoulême joined a group of several hundred knights who, so as to arrive in time for the next Lent, traveled post-haste to Jerusalem. They were not the first, others had preceded them; and Rudolph Glaber tells us in his *Historiarum Libri V* that as the year 1033 drew near "a countless multitude from all parts of the world flocked to the sepulchre of Jesus in Jerusalem; first men of low estate, then men of the middle class, then the great ones of the earth: kings, counts, bishops, prelates. And lastly—this had never been seen before—ladies of the high nobility made their way thither, in the company of people of the humblest rank. Many desired to die before returning to their own land." And, in fact, many did perish on the way. For when these pilgrims set out on that arduous and perilous journey, they hoped it would serve their turn at the moment when the greatest offerings were most needed, in other words when they felt their end approaching. But some of them perished because on their way to the Holy Sepulchre they had to go through countries where Christians of the West were not always welcome. Was it because of the risks involved that pilgrim knights tended to join in armed bands, constantly ready for the fray? Or was it not rather a sign of the combative instinct of a new generation eager to take the measure of its rising strength? In any case this was a decisive moment in the evolution of chivalry vis-à-vis religion.

Until now the Church had shielded herself against the aggressive instincts of the warrior caste, had set up barriers against their intrusions, built ring walls around certain holy places and those groups of the community which most needed protection: clerics, monks, the poor. Now she embarked on a more ambitious plan, that of converting the knights themselves, weaning them from their evil ways, canalizing their restless energy into God's service. A practice developed of fixing Whitsun, the festival commemorating the descent of the Holy Spirit, as the date for the ceremony of initiation into the profession of arms, hitherto a purely pagan rite.

Priests attended it, blessed the young men's swords and assigned to them the tasks which hitherto had been the king's: of protecting the weak and also waging war on the heathens. The first Peace of the Church synods did not prohibit the warriors from fighting; if God had placed them at the apex of the social hierarchy, this was to carry out a military function. But around 1020 some churchmen boldly asserted that "the joys of war" were sinful, that God approved of him who turned his back on them. Thus to the proscriptions of the Pax Ecclesiae were added those of the Truce of God. "From Lent to Easter, I vow never to molest a knight who is unprovided with a weapon of attack." For in the season of penitence it behooved the Christian to abstain from war, no less than from all other carnal pleasures. When, towards the middle of the century, the pilgrimage to St James of Compostela was getting more and more to resemble an armed campaign in Moslem territory, the councils presided over by the bishops went so far as to condemn all acts of violence between Christians. "Let no Christian slay another Christian, for assuredly in so doing he sheds the blood of Christ." Where then were the knights, dedicated as they were to warfare by Divine Providence, to go forth to battle? Surely to lands outside the pale of Christendom, peopled by enemies of the Faith. Thus only a Holy War was lawful. In 1063 the pope urged the knights of Burgundy and Champagne, who were about to make the pilgrimage to Spain, to launch an attack on the infidels; if any of them fell in battle, he, successor of St Peter, guardian of the keys of heaven, promised a plenary indulgence. Fired with holy zeal, the knights took by storm Barbastro, a Saracen town "rich in gold and women." Thirty-five years later another pope proposed a loftier aim to the ardor of the knights: the deliverance of the Holy Sepulchre. To each of the pilgrims-in-arms who rallied to his call he presented the pennon of Christ, emblem of victory. The crusades, indeed, were an outcome of the insistent pressure brought to bear by Christianity on the feudal mentality. What were the first crusaders but the trusty vassals of a jealous God who led the war into the camp of his foes and by dint of mighty blows bent them to His yoke? Among the attributes of divine power figuring in religious sculpture were leather, metal-studded jerkins, hauberks, helmets, shields, a sheaf of lances pointing towards the hosts of darkness.

VIEW OF CONQUES (AVEYRON) WITH THE ABBEY CHURCH OF SAINTE-FOY.

It was about the middle of the tenth century that the Christians in Gaul formed a habit of traveling to Galicia to visit the Roman tomb said to contain the remains of James the Apostle. Henceforth this shrine had an extraordinary attraction for Christian pilgrims, stronger in certain provinces and indeed operative earlier than the appeal of the Holy Sepulchre itself. On the Autun tympanum, recognizable by the shell on his wallet, the pilgrim to Compostela precedes the crusader figure. Along the various roads through the French kingdom converging on this shrine there was an incessant stream of pilgrims which by stimulating exchanges of cultural ideas did much to shape the mentality of eleventh-century man. Though these pilgrimages did not (as once was thought) originate the chansons de geste, *they helped to co-ordinate the subject matter of these verse chronicles, and the masterworks of Romanesque art are to be found along the main pilgrim routes.*

These roads were studded with monasteries where pilgrims could rest on their journey and were lodged according to their social rank in specially equipped "pilgrim-refuges." On leaving, each was given a viaticum. In every abbey on the route they worshipped the relics in it, less highly esteemed no doubt than those of St James, but none the less beneficent. An organized publicity, in which the monasteries excelled, vaunted the specific virtues of these holy objects and drew attention to the frequent miracles attesting their magical power. Compiled under the aegis of Cluny about 1135, the Pilgrims' Guide *advised, for example, "all who go to St James by the Tours route to turn back to venerate at Orléans the wood of the Cross and the chalice of St Euvertius, bishop and confessor, in the church of the Holy Cross; in this same town they must also visit the church of St Samson and see the knife which was undoubtedly the one used at the Last Supper. Also, while on this route the pilgrim must go to the place on the Loire bank where he can gaze on the much-revered body of St Martin, bishop and confessor. There he rests, this most holy saint who miraculously brought back three dead men to life and restored to health lepers, cripples, madmen, demoniacs, and victims of many other diseases. The shrine near the city of Tours which contains his most holy remains glitters with a profusion of gold, silver and precious stones and constant miracles attest its potency." In fact the true divinities of the age were the relics of holy men hidden from the eye under a scintillating mass of goldsmiths' work in the dim religious light of crypts. God—Father, Son and Holy Ghost—remained invisible, but these relics could be touched, they were known to repel the powers of evil, to ward off demons or drive them out of persons* possessed by them, and to counteract the latent infections which covered a man's body with pustules. They were often "mobbed" by wildly excited crowds. At Limoges, for example, "in mid-Lent such a press of people filled the sanctuary for the night services, jostling each other around the tomb of St Martial, that over fifty men and women were crushed to death inside the church."

After a devious path across the Aubrac mountains, pilgrims coming from Notre-Dame-du-Puy arrived at Conques, an abbey that had enjoyed the patronage of the Carolingian kings. Some of its monks had succeeded in a perilous venture, that of securing the relics of St Foy, virgin and martyr, and the fame this brought the monastery was so skilfully exploited, that in the second half of the tenth century a larger church was needed. Odolric, abbot from 1039 to 1065, supervised the building of the new basilica, whose interior layout and decorations made it particularly suitable for the reception—and edification—of large congregations. They gazed in awe at a statue, having the exotic glamour of an African fetish, glittering with gold and gems, within which was contained the skull of the martyred saint. It was reputedly made shortly before the year 1000. "There then prevailed a long-established custom in the regions of Auvergne, Rouergue and Toulouse, and in all nearby lands, of fashioning in each locality, according to its means, a statue of the local saint, reproducing with all due reverence in gold, silver or some other metal the saint's head or some other part of his or her body." These effigies were reminiscent of the anthropomorphic deities which from time immemorial the peasantry had venerated and whose succour they invoked in times of need. These "idols" shocked the master of the cathedral schools of Angers; indeed when he saw them in 1013, this learned man, imbued with the best traditions of Carolingian culture, was startled by this glimpse of another form of Christianity, knowing nothing of intellectual disciplines and all too ready to adjust the Christian ritual to the local superstitions racy of the soil. He even remarked that the decorations of the crypts looked like "reflections of the rites of adoration formerly addressed to pagan gods or, rather, to demons. Ignorant though I am, it seemed to me highly perverse, contrary to all Christian tenets, when for the first time I saw the statue of St Geraldus placed on an altar and given the form of a human face. To most of the peasants who gazed at it in wonder, it seemed to be observing them with an understanding eye and by the impact of its gaze to betoken its acceptance of their prayers."

CHURCH OF SAINTE-FOY, CONQUES (AVEYRON): VAULTING OF THE TRANSEPT CROSSING. 1039-1065.
(CHURCH FINISHED IN THE 12TH CENTURY).

THE BLACK VIRGIN. 11TH CENTURY (?). POLYCHROME WOOD. CHURCH OF DORRES (FRENCH PYRENEES).

OUR LADY OF GOOD HOPE. 11TH CENTURY. POLYCHROME WOOD. CHURCH OF NOTRE-DAME, DIJON.

RELIQUARY STATUE OF SAINTE FOY. 983-1013. ABBEY TREASURE, CONQUES (AVEYRON).

and there, beside the sacred relics of the patron saint, miraculous cures and resurrections took place. Often the relics were surrounded by the tombs of lesser saints, of prelates and princes who had served the monastery well.

The crypt was not only a burial place but a treasure chamber. Amassed around the tombs and relics was a hoard of gold and silver, coins from far-off lands, trinkets, jewels offered by kings of long ago. At the very center of the piety and anxieties of the eleventh century—at the very heart of Romanesque art— stood that masterwork of the goldsmith's art, that gem which the church itself was built to house: the reliquary. A simple box or casket, the reliquary shrine had the form of a sarcophagus whose sides were often discreetly adorned with images in the figural tradition of the imperial workshops. Sometimes it took the form of a tabernacle; such is the small cupboard-like shrine in which Abbot Begon of Conques enclosed the relics received in 1100 from Pope Paschal II. Often, too, the shrine was shaped like the part of the saint's body which it contained; the goldsmith employed by Archbishop Egbert of Trier hammered the metal into the shape of a foot. Its decorations, however, were exclusively classical, for in the late tenth century the episcopal workshop was at the service of the Ottonian emperors, and the influence of the Byzantine renascence made itself felt through the Empress Theophano and her retinue. Finally, in southern Gaul, the reliquary took the form of a statue.

As an instrument of divine grace, the relic was the all-powerful element in the religion of the people. When secular princes presumed to lay violent hands on a church, there was no surer way to subdue and humble them than by taking away the holy relic which gave the church its sacred virtues. The Abbot of Saint-Martial made his way into a church by night: "he took the body of St Vaulry and brought it back with him from Limoges; he kept the relics of this holy confessor until the wicked lords recognized and proclaimed the rights of St Martial; when the saint was restored, not without a heavy payment, to the full possession of his prerogatives, the abbot returned the body to the church from which he had taken it." In times of famine and pestilence, to allay the wrath of God the nobles and the people compelled the priests to bring forth the

DIJON, CRYPT OF THE CATHEDRAL OF SAINT-BÉNIGNE. EARLY 11TH CENTURY.

SHRINE OF ST HADELIN. 12TH CENTURY. CHAMPLEVÉ ENAMELS OF THE SCHOOL OF GODEFROID DE HUY.
CHURCH OF SAINT-MARTIN AT VISÉ, NEAR LIÈGE.

GODEFROID DE HUY:
HEAD-SHRINE OF ST ALEXANDER. STAVELOT, 1145.
MUSÉES ROYAUX D'ART ET D'HISTOIRE, BRUSSELS.
SILVER CHASED AND GILT, INLAID WITH
CHAMPLEVÉ ENAMELS.
OVERALL HEIGHT 17½ IN.

FOOT-SHRINE OF EGBERT,
ARCHBISHOP OF TRIER (977-993).
CATHEDRAL TREASURE, TRIER.

3

THE SAINTS

The monastery churches were nearly always built
over a funerary monument erected in Early Christian
times, the tomb of the monastery's patron saint, a
bishop, confessor or martyr. The Carolingian lands,
where the emperors imposed the liturgical usages
of the Church of Rome, had adopted the type of
church which gave rise to the structural system of the
Romanesque choir and apse. This type of design
was derived from the two-storey structure that Pope
Gregory the Great had raised over the tomb of
St Peter, consisting of two superimposed altars:
at floor level, the altar shrine erected on the tomb
itself; and immediately above it, in a space flooded
with light from the windows, the main altar where
church services took place. Conforming to this
model, the choir of the pilgrimage churches stood
over a crypt. At Tournus and at San Salvador de
Leire the crypt has a basilical plan; that of Saint-
Bénigne of Dijon, built in the time of Abbot William
of Volpiano, has the central plan of a martyry.
In this subterranean chamber were buried the sacred
relics of men and women who had once lived on the
earth but who now in heaven formed part of the
choir invisible and from time to time manifested
their power by laying low those who offended them
and shielding from evil those who feared and
honored them. Through the dim light of the crypt
the monks led processions of awe-stricken pilgrims,

III

THE MONKS

THE WRATH OF GOD

Bristling with weapons, shielded against attack, the western world of the eleventh century lived none the less in a constant state of fear. How be sure that Nature, of which so little was known, might not at any moment unleash her forces against man? While there is no clear trace in any records of a wave of panic in the millennial year, it is certain that Christians felt a very real anxiety as the thousandth anniversary of the Passion approached, the year 1033. The year of God's death counted for more than that of His birth in a society so mindful of the cult of the dead and visits to their tombs. This anniversary, according to the chronicler Rudolph Glaber, was preceded by a series of catastrophes. "Men thought that the order of the seasons and elements which had reigned since the beginning of time had been destroyed, chaos had come again and the knell of man had tolled." In any case there is good evidence that during this period the undernourished, superstitious peasantry was liable to sudden accesses of terror which, starting in some remote region, spread like wildfire, sending whole villages in headlong flight across the countryside.

At the source of the rankling disquiet leading to these panics lay a belief in the imminence of the Last Day. "The world is growing old"—these words often figure in the preamble of deeds of gift to religious foundations. But everyone wished to know in advance the date assigned to this dreadful happening when the world would "shrivel like a parched scroll." With this in mind schoolmen searched the Scriptures. In the Book of Revelation (Chapter XX) they read that Satan was to be loosed from his prison and the horsemen of the Apocalypse would spread havoc in the four quarters of the earth "when the thousand years are expired." On this text was based the forecast of the preacher who, towards the middle of the tenth century, "announced to the congregation of a church in Paris that Antichrist would come at the end of the year 1000 and that shortly after his coming the Last Judgment would

take place." Nevertheless many clerics discouraged speculations of this kind; it was most unseemly, they said, to pry into the secrets of the Most High, nor was it lawful to forecast the day and hour He alone had ordained. No explicit mention of a date was to be found in the Gospels; only of premonitory signs. "Nation shall rise against nation, and kingdom against kingdom: and there shall be famines and pestilences, and earthquakes in divers places. All these are the beginning of sorrows." Then will be the time for men to make ready to confront the dazzling brightness of the face of Christ, coming down from heaven to judge the living and the dead. And in the millennial year the whole Christian world kept anxious watch for these premonitory signs.

What did men know of the structure of the physical universe? They saw the stars keeping strictly to their courses, dawns and springtimes endlessly recurring, all creatures moving irreversibly from birth to death. This convinced them that everywhere in the scheme of things God had imposed an order, that stable order exemplified in the walls of Romanesque churches, which their builders took such pains to body forth. Yet sometimes there was a break in these appointed rhythms as if something had gone "out of order." This was the case with such phenomena as meteors and comets (whose orbits were not circular like those of the other celestial bodies), or the monsters seen by mariners, such as the whale "huge as an island which made its appearance at dawn one morning in November, and was seen proceeding on its way until the third hour of the day." What was one to make of cataclysms, unseasonable gales, volcanic eruptions or that dreadful dragon many men saw in the skies of Gaul one Saturday evening before Christmas, "breathing forth vollies of sparks and heading for the South"? Wonders in the air, in the depths of the earth, at sea —descriptions of these happenings fill pages of the chronicles kept up by medieval monks. If they recorded them, it was because they believed these "signs and wonders" were of high significance, celestial warnings of impending doom. During the 1033 eclipse "every man was white as a sheet, all were stricken to the heart with a terror no words can express; for well they knew it to be a portent of some terrible disaster that would soon befall mankind." In his description of a comet, Glaber remarks that "as for knowing if this was a new star sent by God or simply a heavenly body whose lustre He had increased so as to strike fear into the hearts of men, these matters concern Him alone whose wisdom rules all things better than words can say. Nevertheless this much is sure: every time men see a portent of this sort on earth or in the heavens, something strange and fearsome soon befalls them." For in the world-view common to all, even the erudite, the universe was pictured as a gigantic forest, trackless, "measureless to man." To penetrate it, to ward against its hidden perils, the wisest course was to act like the skilled hunter: to follow a winding path, to study faintly indicated traces and take guidance from a pattern of seemingly haphazard coincidences. Was it not clear that the order of the scheme of things rested on a network of slender links charged with magical properties? Anything perceptible to the senses—a word, a gesture, a noise, a lightning flash—might be a sign. Only by patiently unraveling the tangled skein of phenomena could man hope to make a little progress, to blaze a trail in the dark forest of the natural world.

At the very heart of the mystery he had glimpses of strange events that needed skilled interpretation. The great thing was to trace their origin: which of the unknown, stealthy forces lurking behind the veil of appearances had given rise to them? Were they the work of chthonic powers, those furtive emissaries of Satan, hordes of which, to the thinking of medieval man, lay in wait beneath the earth and in the undergrowth, seeking whom they might devour: those hideous creatures—half snake, half woman—conjured up to such grim effect by the Romanesque artists? "It is common knowledge that wars and whirlwinds, pestilences, all the evils that afflict the human race are the work of devils." Christianization had imposed on the complex of ideas inherited by eleventh-century man a certain number of images and tenets, but had never really succeeded in effacing the belief-patterns of the past: that mythological deposit in which for untold generations men had sought to find an explanation of the unknowable.

These mental images tended towards a crude manichaeism envisaging the universe as the scene of an endless duel between Good and Evil, between God and rebel hosts that resented His order and disarranged it. Hence the belief that all catastrophes, sudden breaks in the divinely ordained rhythm were defeats of the friendly forces, victories of man's arch-enemy, the devil, whom an angel had held captive "for the space of one thousand years" and who was now breaking loose, attacking and spreading ruin, like the wanton knights who galloping across the fields trampled down the rising crops.

But why not take the opposite view: that God Himself, not Satan, sent these signs? An irascible God, prone to fly into a rage, like the kings of the earth when they felt themselves braved or betrayed, yet a God who loved His children, who preferred to warn them in advance rather than strike them unexpectedly, and to give them breathing-space in which to prepare themselves for His hardest blows. All his life long man is crushed by the Almighty's power, but he must never lose heart. His Creator has given him eyes to see and ears to hear, and speaks to him as Jesus spoke to the disciples, in parables. He uses obscure metaphors and it is the Christian's duty to seek out their meaning. By the startling deviations He introduces into the normal course of events He does humanity the service of putting it on its guard. These are preliminary warnings of the sterner punishment to come. The manifold disasters that befell the peasantry in the year 1000—floods, war, plague and famine—were natural enough in a still extremely backward civilization always at the mercy of the weather, epidemic disease, outbreaks of demented violence. All these inexplicable phenomena were taken to be the great tribulations spoken of by St Matthew as heralding the Son of man's "coming in the clouds of heaven" for the Last Judgment, and as such a call to repentence.

Admittedly the only data telling us of the climate of opinion in the eleventh century are furnished by documents which, written in monasteries, were given a didactic slant. They were recorded by men whose vocation inclined them to pessimism and to regarding renouncement of the world as the ideal rule of life. Naturally enough the monks exhorted others to undergo the privations they had imposed on themselves, and their preaching was fortified by the signs and wonders taking place in ever greater numbers: tokens of God's displeasure. In fact there was every indication of the nearness of Christ's Second Coming and the Last Day. To enter the banqueting hall to which the heavenly King would shortly summon them all men must don in haste the "wedding garment," and woe to him who was not thus attired! Let each man, then, cleanse himself of the taint of sin and, willingly rejecting carnal pleasures, earn God's indulgence. There is every indication that the widely attended gatherings whose ostensible purpose was to make good the Peace of God in southern Gaul were in reality penitential assemblies convened with a view to collective purification. An epidemic of ergotic poisoning in Aquitaine was regarded as a manifestation of God's wrath. At Limoges "the bodies and relics of saints were brought in from all directions and the body of St Martial, patron saint of Gaul, was exhumed from its sepulchre. All men rejoiced exceedingly, everywhere the disease abated, while the Duke and the nobility joined in a pact of peace and justice."

This will to peace and concord had a part in the movement towards austerity activated by the premonitory signs of the Last Day. For the vows to keep the Peace of God bade all good Christians eschew the "joys" of combat. And at the same time as the Church was imposing on the knights, as the penitence most befitting their estate, the periodical abstention from warfare known as the Truce, she stiffened the rules of fasting. For surely the priests whose duty it was to provide a model of the Christian life should set the example by practising purity and chastity, renouncing the luxuries indulged in by the knights, and above all getting rid of their concubines—in short behave like monks. To win God's mercy, to be made ready for the Second Coming, all taints of sin must be wiped out, more heed be given to the basic prohibitions. Satan keeps his votaries in thrall by playing on men's lusts: for gold, for war, for rich food and for women.

Let all, now that the hour of Judgment is at hand, resist these four temptations. The renunciation of wealth, the laying down of arms, a life of continence, the custom of fasting—none of them was new, the monks had practised these abstentions for centuries. So the Church now bade every Christian imitate the monks, observe the same rules of poverty, chastity, peace and temperance and turn his back on all things carnal. Thus, at last united in the Faith, the whole human race would make its way to the New Jerusalem clad in the austere habit of the coenobites.

Convinced that the End of the World was at hand, the eleventh century took for its ideal —an ideal which works of art were called on to evoke—the way of life obtaining in the monasteries. Situated in the heart of great empty spaces where only a few acres had been rescued from the forest, surrounded by a peasantry bowed down by endless toil and the prey of atavistic fears, and built beside castles manned by the rude warriors of medievaldom, the monasteries too were strongholds, but strongholds with a difference: oases of hope and piety against which the powers of evil launched their attacks in vain. To the thinking of the age the Christian community had two lines of defence and was guarded by two allied orders: the order of those who carried arms and the order of those who prayed. And where could men pray better than in the refuges of purity protected by the cloister walls? Day after day in all the abbeys of the West a host of worshippers offered, like Abel, to God the only sacrifices to which, as to Abel's, the Lord "had respect." The monks had more power than the enfeebled kings of Europe, than bishops and priests, of averting the divine wrath; in the domain of religion they were clearly paramount. The knighthood, firmly entrenched in Latin Christendom, might have the upper hand in worldly affairs. But in the affairs of the spirit, in the domain of religious fears and supernature—and by the same token in creative art—the monks held unquestioned sway.

"Let nothing be ranked higher than the divine service": the Bene-dictine Rule gave a central place in monastic life to the ceremony of praise to God. Its choral prayers, processions and elaborate ritual fell into two concentric cycles. The intoning of the psalms never ceased throughout the day. In the hours of darkness a bell summoned the monks for the night service; this was followed successively by Lauds, a hymn to God chanted at daybreak, and Prime, said when the sun was rising. In the hours of daylight, when the monks had their daily tasks like other men, the canonical hours—Terce, Sext and None—were shorter. But collective prayers began again at the approach of night; at Compline all the monks joined in prayers for protection against the perils of the night.

The other cycle, covering the year, centered on Easter. One of the main duties of the sacrist and precentor, the monks responsible for the conduct of the services, was to compile the Calendar for the Year, to distribute the books appointed to be read and to organize the services enjoined on special days. Thus the life of prayer involved a constant awareness of the unbroken course of Time, whose cyclic rhythms it observed punctiliously, and by refusing to countenance any interruption in them the monastic community lived already in eternity. The monks could truly say that, for them, death was vanquished. There was no break of continuity; the living friars prayed for the dead, as if they were still present at their sides. The eternal return of the daily and yearly prayers did away with any notion of a personal destiny, of youth or age. This explains why the symbolism of the movements of the heavenly bodies was given a central place in monastic art.

The Gerona tapestry, like the Bayeux tapestry, belongs to a type of monumental decoration very few examples of which have survived, but which, none the less, had a major role among the accessories of divine worship. The walls of Romanesque churches have come down to us bare of any decoration, and we like them thus. But, when new, they were embellished with frescoes, oftener with figured textiles. In the eleventh century Amalfi owed its wealth wholly to the importation of silk fabrics from the East. These were not used as yet for personal adornment, except by kings and high-ranking prelates who wore them at public ceremonies in which they sought to evoke for the edification of the populace the hieratic splendors of the celestial world. They were mostly used for draping walls. When Pope Celestine II made his state entry into Benevento, "the whole town was clad in purple," and as a gift to the Emperor Henry IV, Desiderius, Abbot of Monte Cassino, bought from traders at Amalfi "twenty pieces of most rare, truly imperial silk."

THE FLIGHT INTO EGYPT. 1004-1030.
CAPITAL IN THE NARTHEX, CHURCH OF SAINT-BENOÎT-SUR-LOIRE, NEAR ORLÉANS.

NOLI ME TANGERE. 12TH CENTURY. CAPITAL IN THE CHURCH OF SAINT-ANDOCHE, SAULIEU, NEAR DIJON.

THE SIGNS OF THE LION AND THE RAM. FIRST HALF OF THE 12TH CENTURY.
MARBLE FIGURES FROM THE CHURCH OF SAINT-SERNIN, TOULOUSE. MUSÉE DES AUGUSTINS, TOULOUSE.

THE DESCENT FROM THE CROSS. 12TH CENTURY. RELIEF ON THE NORTHEAST PILLAR,
CLOISTER OF SANTO DOMINGO DE SILOS, NEAR BURGOS.

FULDA SACRAMENTARY: THE MONTHS (CALENDAR PAGE). LAST THIRD OF THE 10TH CENTURY.
STAATSBIBLIOTHEK, BERLIN (ON LOAN TO THE STAATSBIBLIOTHEK, TÜBINGEN, THEOL. LAT. FOLIO 192).

GERONA TAPESTRY: THE CREATION, DETAIL. ABOUT 1100.
CATHEDRAL TREASURE, GERONA, SPAIN.

4

THE MONASTERY

Western Europe in the eleventh century still had its hermits, men who elected to live a solitary life of penance in remote caves and fens, after the manner of the anchorites of the Greek Church; and many of them were to be found in out-of-the-way corners of Italy. But most monks lived together in fraternal communities, like the apostles. Under the Rule of St Benedict, the bond of brotherhood was even closer than ties of blood among high-born knights, and the monastery was like the domain of a large and prosperous family with a vast estate and many servants. It had contacts with the outside world: on its threshold stood buildings set aside for hospitality and charity, where pilgrims and the poor were housed and fed; near the hostelry were quarters for the servants charged with the menial tasks which the monks, devoting themselves entirely to their liturgical office, no longer had time to perform; and to the gate-house of the monastery came peasants with the produce of their labors in the fields, and the surplus of their abundant contributions was stored away in the cellars and granaries. But very few monks were to be seen at this point of contact with the outside world and its temptations. As a rule they lived in cloistered isolation, cut off from the world by a wall which they had vowed never to cross. The monastery was a closed community, self-sufficing and self-contained.

POMPOSA (NEAR FERRARA), FAÇADE AND TOWER OF THE MONASTERY CHURCH. 10TH-12TH CENTURY.

CLUNY (BURGUNDY), THE ABBEY CHURCH SEEN FROM BEHIND THE APSE.
FROM A LITHOGRAPH BY EMILE SAGOT (AFTER 1798). CABINET DES ESTAMPES, BIBLIOTHÈQUE NATIONALE, PARIS.

Of that renunciation which was the first principle of the religious life, the cloister was a symbolic representation. It was a place of retirement and seclusion. Its proportions were so designed as to body forth perfections which are not of this world. A quadrilateral co-ordinated with the four cardinal points and the four elements of the cosmos, the cloister was a small space shielded from the evils to which human life since the Fall has been a prey, and recreated in terms of the "divine quaternity," paragon of perfection, spoken of by Rudolph Glaber. For the man who withdrew to the cloister, everything around him breathed intimations of the life to come in the Other World.

The church itself communicated directly with the dormitory, since the monks held divine services during the night. St Benedict thought of the monastery church as a private oratory. "After divine service, all the friars will file out in profound silence and they will show to God the reverence which is His due; so that if a friar should wish to tarry and spend a while in solitary prayer, he will not be troubled by the importunity of others. Likewise, should a monk at any other time desire to say his orisons in private, let him be free to go in and pray." The monastery church was originally intended for the exclusive use of the monastic community; as a rule no outsiders were admitted. But in fact the abbey churches had opened their doors to pilgrims during the eleventh century. This was in response to the pressure of the masses, eager for miracles and initiation into the secrets of the Other World. Moreover, as a result of ecclesiastical reforms, new monasteries were being created around the older basilicas which, founded on the tombs of saints and staffed by teams of prelates, the canons, had been and now continued to be centers of popular worship. Finally, as the cult of relics spread, the Benedictine abbeys themselves acquired holy relics and became shrines to which the faithful flocked. The role of the monastery was thus gradually being changed—until Cîteaux reacted against this tendency.

Hardly any trace remains today of the monastic buildings erected in the eleventh century; like the homes of even the greatest lords, they were flimsily constructed. In most cases only the church still stands. For at this time the monks, whenever possible, rebuilt their churches in stone. From about 1000 on, building projects were in progress in all parts of Christian Europe, and the monks and churchmen, with their master-masons, proceeded to devise a new style of religious architecture. The boldest innovations were made in the eastern Pyrenees and in Burgundy. Oliva, abbot of Ripoll and Cuxa, seems to have been the moving spirit of the new Catalan architecture, from which stemmed the church of Saint-Martin-du-Canigou, begun in 1001, and the admirable ensemble of San Pedro de Roda, consecrated in 1022. Their counterparts in Burgundy were Tournus, Saint-Bénigne of Dijon, and above all Cluny. As early as 955 work had begun on a church that was to replace the first oratory of Cluny. Consecrated in 981, this edifice was given a barrel vault that improved its acoustics, enhancing the rich sonorities of the liturgic plainsong. In the second half of the eleventh century the builders of Payerne and Romainmôtier (now in Switzerland, but then part of the kingdom of Burgundy) drew inspiration from it, as did the Norman monks whom William of Volpiano had recently reformed, also the German monks of Hirsau. But this second Cluny church was soon torn down to make place for another, still larger and more grandiose, the third church of Cluny.

This last was destroyed early in the nineteenth century (it had gradually fallen into complete ruin), but enough has survived to demonstrate the immense size of the monastery, built to house a very large religious fraternity. In 1088, when the abbot St Hugh started work on it, the community numbered over three hundred monks. At first building proceeded rapidly, for alms flowed in abundantly from many sources. In 1095 Pope Urban II, a former Cluniac monk, consecrated the high altar, in the course of the missionary journey which took him to Clermont to preach the first crusade. But then work slowed down and the vault collapsed in 1125. Six years later Pope Innocent II solemnized a rededication, but for many years the abbots lacked the funds needed to complete the church. The truth is that Abbot Hugh had "seen big," had made plans for a building some 600 feet long with exceptionally high vaults, so that his sons, escaping from the prison-like seclusion of the cloister, could let their thoughts soar freely towards the celestial heights. An image of heaven, the basilica had better lighting than any other Romanesque church. "Full of the glory of God, it was like a gathering place of angels."

PAYERNE (SWITZERLAND), NAVE OF THE ABBEY CHURCH. 10TH-12TH CENTURY.

ABBEY OF SAINT-MARTIN-DU-CANIGOU, PYRENEES.
BUILT BETWEEN 1001-1009 AND 1026.

MONASTERY OF SAN PEDRO DE RODA, NEAR GERONA, CATALONIA.
10TH-11TH CENTURY.

MOISSAC (NEAR TOULOUSE), CLOISTER OF THE CHURCH OF SAINT-PIERRE. FINISHED IN 1100.

THE FUNCTIONS
OF THE MONASTERY

A society that attributed so much value to set formulas and gestures and lived in constant apprehension of the unseen world needed rites to still its ghostly fears and to make its peace with the supernatural powers; it called for sacraments and, therefore, priests. Still more necessary seemed the duty to "pray without ceasing." These prayers took the form of liturgical chants rising in clouds of incense towards the throne of God, sounding His praises and entreating His mercy. Hence the need for monks.

Their primary function was to pray for the community as a whole. For at that time the individual did not count, he was a mere unit in a group, all personal initiatives were merged completely into the activities and collective obligations of the community. Just as the vengeance of a family was a joint enterprise in which all its members took part and reprisals were directed not only against the offender but also against all his kinsmen, so the whole body of believers felt responsible, in God's eyes, for the acts of each of its members; tainted by the crime that one of them committed, purified by the holiness of others. For most men saw themselves as too paltry or too ignorant to achieve salvation by their unaided efforts. Or, rather, they hoped to win redemption by a sacrifice performed by others, whereby the whole community benefited and whose merit succored all alike. The agents of this communal redemption were the monks. The monastery acted as an intermediary in spiritual matters; it procured God's pardon and dispensed it to others. True, the monks were the first to benefit by these direct dealings with their heavenly Lord; by prayer and fasting they staked a personal claim on the celestial fief which was to reward their loyal service; nevertheless other men shared in the divine favor thus acquired—and the more abundantly, the closer were their contacts with the monastic community. In their devotions the monks gave priority to intercessions for their next-of-kin. This explains why so many scions of the nobility were dedicated

to the service of God in early youth and sent to an abbey where all their life they would pray for the spiritual welfare of their kinsmen who had remained in the outside world. But the monks also labored for the salvation of all their "brothers in the spirit" and this is why so many laymen affiliated themselves to a monastery, by the donation of their persons, by an act of vassalage, or by joining one of the many pious confraternities which sprang up around every church. And, finally, the monks made a point of doing their utmost for the salvation of their benefactors; hence the frequency of gifts made to the monasteries. These are among the reasons why so many monasteries were founded and prospered at this time; most of them for men (there were few nunneries) as was to be expected in a culture so thoroughly masculine, in which the question was often asked, "Have women a soul?" Such being the primordial functions of the monasteries, we can understand why a large part of their income was devoted to decorative enterprises. For the praises of the Lord are not celebrated by prayers alone; they call for offerings of things of beauty, of ornaments, of the types of architecture most suitable for bodying forth the omnipotence of the Lord God. So it was that the decline of monarchical power and changes in the social system led to a transference to the abbeys of the hitherto royal function of consecration and that of sponsoring artistic ventures. Indeed the flowering of sacred art in the eleventh century was largely due to monks and their desire to embellish the offices of the church.

Moreover, the monasteries had now become repositories of relics. No layman had dared as yet to keep in his possession these remains of sacred bodies, charged with such tremendous power: numinous manifestations of the supernatural in the world of men. Only the king, or else those holy men, the monks had the right to lay hands on them. The edifice housing them was always the property of a saint, their patron; he would not suffer any ordinary mortal to touch them, the fires of God would strike down any man who trespassed on his rights. Christ himself was physically present in some of these relics, vestiges of His earthly sojourn; thus they created a link between the everyday world and the mystery of the unseen. It was close beside the relics of a saint or martyr that the Christian best paid homage to him, could feel certain of his miraculous protection, and count most surely on his help in an hour of need, for any of the maladies whose course he governed, or on the brink of death. Many abbeys were built above the tombs of martyrs or famous missionaries, heroes of the incessant war with the powers of darkness. On one tomb, or on several. At Saint-Germain of Auxerre, "in the small church there were no less than twenty-two altars," and Rudolph Glaber when renovating the epitaphs of the saints "adorned in like manner the sepulchres of certain religious notables." Supervisors of the cult of relics, celebrated in shadowy crypts among sarcophagi, the monks served as mediators between the underground world of the dead and the world of the living. This, their basic function, had a marked effect on art. For it involved the disposition around the relics of ornaments worthy of their virtues. The monastery church itself became a monumental reliquary invested with all the splendor feasible in that age. And, being concerned with the relics of dead saints, it naturally had affinities with funerary art.

This preoccupation with death characteristic of eleventh-century Christianity testifies to the continuing vigor of certain beliefs which, long current in the lower strata of the populace, had been reactivated by the triumph of feudality. By encouraging their adoption by the Church the feudal lords elevated these beliefs to the highest cultural level and they were given a new lease of life. All the legends basic to the medieval verse chronicles took their rise in the vicinity of cemeteries, such as the Alyscamps at Arles and at Vézelay (tomb of Girart of Roussillon) at the time when Christian burial rites were undergoing a modification. Formerly these had simply entrusted the dead man, with all his sins upon him, to the mercy of God. Now, however, the knighthood bade its priests take steps to sanctify the corpse; hence the insertion into the funeral rite of the act of censing and formulas of absolution —implying that the priest himself had the power of remitting sins. For the dead body's sojourn until the day of resurrection no place could be more salu-

tary than one in the vicinity of sacred relics and of the choir where constantly the priest voiced supplications to the God of Judgment. This is why graveyards proliferated around the monasteries, the most favored and costliest places in them being those adjoining the church wall. Funeral services held on the graves came to bulk ever larger in the liturgy and day after day an ever-lengthening list of names of those for whom a special mass was to be celebrated figured in the obituary notices. Last but not least, the monastery welcomed men on the point of death. A practice grew up among the knights of being "converted," i.e. changing their way of life on their deathbed and donning the Benedictine habit. Thus in the hour of death they joined the community of monks and won a place in that spiritual lineage which would never end and, mindful of the salvation of all its members, would pray for them year in, year out. At the Last Judgment, it was hoped, the resurrected man, closely surrounded by his brothers the monks, might, if all went well, succeed in concealing from the divine Judge's eyes a garment less immaculate than theirs. Envisaged as collective graveyards forming a halfway stage between the drab reality of earth and the splendors of heaven, the abbey churches were bedecked with all the beauties of the world.

Shrines, cemeteries, founts of indulgences, monasteries were so essential that more and more were built. But for their ministrations to take full effect, assurance of their complete integrity and independence was indispensable. Now, as it so happened, monachism had suffered greatly in the troubles of the ninth and tenth centuries. Stocked with treasures but ill defended, the abbeys were the first points attacked by bands of pillagers. They had been looted and burnt by Northmen, Saracens and Hungarians and the monks compelled to take to flight. Violently expelled from their seclusion, they had been abruptly cast adrift in the outside world, domain of the Evil One, and exposed defencelessly to the temptations of the age. Most of them ended up by establishing new foundations, in provinces less liable to heathen attacks. Thus, after long wanderings the community of Noirmoutier, driven on and on by the Vikings, succeeded in carrying to Tournus, on the Saône, the relics of St Philibert, their patron, and in building at this peaceful spot one of the finest abbey churches in the "new style." But in the same period the monasteries were forced to bow to another yoke.

The kings, once their patrons, were losing hold of them. In the year 1000, in the diocese of Noyon, close though it was to the royal residences of the Capetians, only one of the seven abbeys was still under the patronage of the king of France; all the others had gradually come under the personal control of local princes. Meanwhile numerous members of the high nobility, and others less highly placed, mere castle-owners, founded monasteries in which to "place" some of their sons, bury their dead, and have prayers said for their well-being in this world and the next. And since the founder of a monastery regarded it as his private property, the monks soon came to be treated by him like the serfs included in a family inheritance. They were under the strict control of a master who ruthlessly exploited them and kept to himself the offerings made by worshippers at the shrines. Often, too, he squandered the treasure of the monastery church, drew on it for feeding his packs of hounds and paying the upkeep of his concubines, and compelled the friars to make do with the crumbs that fell from the great man's table. Even where better treated the monks were obliged to transfer in fiefs to their patron's knights much of the monastery's domain and feed his henchmen in their refectory. However independent he might seem, every abbot, every prior was harassed by temporal problems, constrained to lodge complaints against nearby lords who were challenging the saint's rights. Sometimes he had no choice but to make war on them and enterprises of this kind, coupled with the turbulence of the feudal age, led to frequent lapses from the Christian's proper path. How, then, apply the Rule, maintain respect for the cloistered life and save the monks from the taint of bloodshed common to warriors, their greed for gold, their fleshly lusts? How keep up the monastic standard of erudition in these conditions?

Once the West had emerged from a state of chaos and spiritual darkness, its rulers applied themselves to restoring the instruments of collective prayer; this was to their mind the most urgent task. Some members of the nobility took the lead. Anxious, at the close of their lives, to win the favor of heaven, they strove to restore order in the monasteries founded by their ancestors, or those whose patronage they had taken over from the kings. In 980 the reform movement, which had begun in the early years of the tenth century, was in full swing and by 1140 it had achieved its object. The functions then assumed by the monastic communities show that this spirit of reform developed, primarily, in the abbeys. Until the beginning of the twelfth century the official Church remained tied up with temporal affairs; this explains why in the period we are here concerned with abbots were more esteemed than bishops, and the monks triumphed everywhere. Because they led holier lives and the services they rendered God were clearly of a higher quality. This was the underlying reason for the success of monachism that Adalberon, Bishop of Laon, deplored in a conversation with Robert the Pious. Until 1140 the great centers of Western culture, the places where the new art was given form, were not cathedrals but monasteries. For the latter were built in the heart of the country at the center of some great domain that, having benefited by the steady advance in agricultural methods, was better adapted to the acquirements and activities of an essentially rural society. But the chief reason for this primacy was that the monastic institutions had been renovated much earlier, cleansed of the blemishes that for a while had marred their spiritual health. In western medievaldom abbots were canonized sooner than bishops, quicker to provide educational facilities, less inclined to squander the ever increasing wealth provided by almsgiving, and devoted it to rebuilding and adorning abbey churches.

The reformer of a monastic establishment was usually some highly gifted man, famed for the strictness of his morals and his energy, whom feudal princes, wishing to have the best type of monks in their domains, called in to eradicate indiscipline. This man of God moved from place to place in his crusade for better morals in the monasteries. To safeguard his reforms he retained control of several of the houses he had reorganized. They formed a united group under his orders and, by reason of their union, were better able to resist any recrudescence of the evils with which they had been afflicted and, more important still, any attempts by the secular power to intermeddle in their affairs. Thus the reform gave rise in the natural course of events to the "congregation," that is to say a structure which henceforth determined many of the traits of sacred art. Until recently art historians dealing with Romanesque productions divided them up by provinces and spoke, for example, of a Provençal or a Poitou school. But the notable resemblances between certain eleventh-century monuments were much less due to proximity than to certain spiritual affinities that in all parts of Christendom linked together the monasteries which, having been reorganized by the same reformer, had subsequently kept in close touch with each other. Often their abbots demonstrated these affinities by building churches of the same type and similarly decorated.

There were many groups of this kind. Among them mention may be made of the one which took form in Lorraine on the initiative of Richard of St Vanne and of the Mediterranean foundation which affiliated under the aegis of the church of Saint-Victor at Marseilles a number of Catalan and Sardinian monasteries. Another group was formed by William of Volpiano, abbot of Saint-Bénigne at Dijon, when in 1001 the Duke of Normandy asked him "to set on the right path" the monks at Fécamp; in 1003 he founded Fruttuaria in Lombardy. This abbot owed his success to his extreme severity, he was said to be punctilious *super regulam*, demanding even more than the Rule required: "mortification of the flesh, abjection of the body, squalid garments, scanty nourishment." He imposed on the monks a strict asceticism calculated to keep them in a state of the utmost purity and to make their prayers "more agreeable to the Lord." Along the axis of his original ministrations—running from northern Italy to the English Channel—branches proliferated; the reform movement spread from Fécamp to the abbey of Saint-Ouen at Rouen, to Bernay, Jumièges, Saint-Michel-au-péril-de-la-mer (invoked by Roland at the hour of his death, since to the archangel Michael fell the task of weighing souls on Judgment Day) and a number of monasteries on which William the Conqueror and Lanfranc drew after 1066 in order to provide England with good bishops, and where the most eminent divines of the year 1100, among others St Anselm, were trained. The influence of Dijon made itself felt in Bèze, Septfontaines, Saint-Michel of Tonnerre and Saint-Germain of Auxerre (where Rudolph Glaber was a monk); that of Fruttuaria extended to the monastery of Sant' Ambrogio at Milan and Sant'Apollinare at Ravenna. When he died in 1031 William was abbot in sole control of no less than forty houses and over twelve hundred monks.

But towering above all other congregations of the eleventh-century was the Order of Cluny. Founded in 910, the abbey enjoyed complete independence, neither the temporal powers nor even bishops were permitted to meddle in its affairs. With this in view its founder had linked it directly to the Church of Rome, whose patron saints, Peter and Paul, it shared. It was certainly to this total autonomy—the monks had the right to elect their own abbot, unaffected by any outside pressure—that the success of the Cluniac Order was due. In 980, though already vastly respected, it still was modest in its ambitions; Maieul, its abbot, refused to reform Fécamp and Saint-Maur-des-Fossés and delegated this duty to one of his disciples, William of Volpiano. The Cluniac "empire" was created by St Odilo around the year 1000. He induced a great number of smaller houses to place themselves under the control of a single abbot and to adopt the Cluny style of monachism, the *ordo cluniensis*; the Holy See directly encouraged this move by granting to all the daughter houses special privileges: immunity as regards the lay lords and exemptions vis-à-vis the bishops. The Order steadily gained ground on both sides of the frontier between the French kingdom and the Empire, ramifying into Burgundy, Provence and Aquitaine. Then it established itself in those parts of the West which were most emancipated from the domination of the monarchs, that is to say where the process of feudalization had been carried furthest and the stabilizing factor was the Peace of God; and in the provinces where latinity had not been grafted on to the prevailing culture by Court archaeologists, but was a natural growth deeply rooted in the soil—in other words the true domain of Romanesque aesthetic. By way of the pilgrim route of Compostela the Cluniac system penetrated Spain and its establishment in the great royal monastery of San Juan de la Peña led the Spanish Church to adopt the Roman rites. In 1077 the King of England installed a Cluniac foundation at Lewes and two years later the King of France founded another in Paris, the monastery of Saint-Martin-des-Champs. Not only did the congregation have branches in countries where monarchical art held sway, but it also won favor with the greatest sovereigns of the West. The King of Castile presented it with the Arab gold coins that circulated freely south of the Pyrenees; the King of England with the silver that was pouring into the North Sea ports thanks to the prosperity of seaborne trade. These precious metals helped to rebuild the abbey church and to adorn it on a scale worthy of the huge organization over which Cluny had control. The Cluniac system owed allegiance neither to a king nor to the emperor; it was self-sufficient. And though the monks of Cluny saw in Alfonso of Castile and Henry of England the true founders of the Order, its moving spirit was Abbot Hugh, friend of the Emperor, adviser to the Pope, and by general consent the guiding spirit of Christendom.

The reformed monks of Lorraine accepted the rule of their bishops and these prelates, who were selected by the Emperor, were then the best—or should one say "the least bad"?—to be found in Europe. On the other hand, in the provinces where Cluny had a foothold the inroads of feudalism had thrown the secular Church administration so completely out of gear that the Cluniac movement had to make an open stand against the bishops. It disintegrated the dioceses at the same time as the growing insubordination of lords of castles was disintegrating the countships. Thus the triumph of Cluny coincided with the decline of the episcopate and a progressive deterioration of the Carolingian system in which the reins of government had been held conjointly by the bishop and the count, under the guidance of the sovereign. This triumph also involved a setback of the cathedral schools, a weakening of the humanistic tendencies due to a study of the Latin classics, and by the same token a retrogression of the "royal" aesthetic. On the intellectual plane, in the domain of religious thought and artistic creation, the conquests of Cluny parallel-ed those of feudalism; indeed they joined forces in destroying the tradition of the previous age. This widespread renovation which, starting from Cluny and the region of its earliest successes, gradually spread all over Europe (it coincides exactly with the extension of the forms of art we now call Roman-esque) submerged the Carolingian heritage. Little by little it became obliterated, leaving the field free for indigenous forces, welling up from the Roman substratum, to make their full effect.

Together with the less spectacular but very real advance of rural economy, the success of Cluny was an epochal event in eleventh-century European history, far-reaching and complete. Bishop Aldabe-ron wrote a whole poem devoted to proving to the king of France that the victories of the "black-habited militia" were undermining his power. Cluny owed its success to the exceptional ability of four abbots whose administration of the great monastery demonstrated that a religious institution could per-fectly fulfill the duties the lay world expected of it. "Know," wrote Rudolph Glaber, "that this House hath not its equal in the Roman world, above all in the task of rescuing souls that have come into Satan's clutches... In this monastery, as I have seen with my own eyes, so great is the number of monks that it is customary for masses to be said without an instant's break from the peep of day until the hour of sleep, and such was the dignity, such the piety pervading them, one could well believe that the officiants were not men but angels." For concomi-tantly with its insistence on asceticism (all the more necessitated by the imminence of the end of the world) Cluny stressed the need for thorough-going purity, and combined the administration of the sacraments, function of the priesthood, with the austerities of the monastic life. By contrast the world-liness, not to say frivolity, of the ordained priests became yet more glaring. The triumph of Cluny held out hopes of that universalization of monachism of which the bishops of Aquitaine dreamt when the year of the millennium of the Passion approached and the world was racked by calamities and epide-mics. But Cluny also succeeded—and this was per-haps the chief reason of its immense influence—in meeting the desires of a populace haunted by the fear of death. Nowhere to finer effect than in the great Burgundian abbey were celebrated the funer-ary rites, the masses for the dead and the memorial repasts at which the whole community of monks joined in celebrating the memory of a dead man and making propitiatory libations. To the Cluniac abbots was due the practice of combining in one service, the second of November, the commemoration of all the dead. They declared that souls would be deli-vered sooner from the pains of purgatory if certain specified prayers were made on their behalf. They also carried out an extensive program of thoroughly Christianizing the naive, semi-pagan beliefs touching the future life that had lingered on among the lower classes, all the daughter houses of the Order being enlisted in this missionary enterprise. This is why so many of the greatest princes of Europe desired to be buried in the graveyard of the parent monastery. The basilica of Cluny, which undoubtedly repre-sented all that was best in eleventh-century art and whose elements and ornaments were devised to sig-nify the resurrection of the dead to the sound of the trumpets of the Second Coming, in a blaze of light, rose from a soil fertilized by a multitude of graves.

The art we know as Romanesque found its supreme expression in architecture. For the chief concern of artistic creation in the eleventh century was the building of churches, edifices in which divine service could be celebrated with the utmost splendor and in whose very structure the major symbols of the Faith were embodied. Combined with the art of music that of architecture sought to make perceptible to the human senses the order of the universe and the attributes of God. Painting and sculpture could never give more than intimations of the supernal world, whereas the edifice could body forth its entire significance. Its function was to co-operate in the revelation of the divine and, like the liturgy, like close study of the Scriptures and meditation on them, to help the monks gradually to apprehend the inexpressible by its structure, an organized arrangement of meaningful elements. For the church purported to be a plenary representation both of the cosmos and of man the microcosm: in other words of all Creation. Thus it conveyed an image of God Himself, since by His will there existed a resemblance between Him and His creatures.

This image had already been provided in the Romanesque cathedral by the manner of its disposition in space. Oriented eastwards, it caught the first sunbeams marking the ending of the night and the terrors that walk in darkness, and this reassuring light of daybreak was greeted in the cycle of the liturgy by a hymn of praise to the Creator. Thus the church was turned, symbolically, towards a realm of hope, that of a glorious resurrection, and the position it occupied relatively to the four cardinal points imposed on the processions of monks a direction towards the blaze of light announcing the Second Coming. The ground plan, too, was a sign. It was largely determined by exigencies of the ritual; the parallel aisles, staircases, ambulatories and the exits provided by the transepts—all were designed to facilitate the ritual, the access of pilgrims to the relics, the movements of the monks from their cells in the cloisters to the places where they prayed. Thus the layout of the church was functional, its structure adapted to the program of the collective worship taking place in it. But it was also symbolic. The crossing, forming one of the axes of the basilical plan, and the incurvations of the chevet carried suggestions for the understanding worshipper. For they reminded him of the cross: of both the plain cross of Calvary and the crook of the shepherds of the people. At a deeper level they conveyed an image of man, and of God who created man in His own image, and of the Son of Man in whom the two substances were united. Of man both temporal and spiritual, his arms outspread in the bays of the transept, his head framed in the apse, and the most vital part of his body occupying the choir. The center of the crossing forms a square, as does the cloister. Its shape signifies the four elements of the terrestrial world and the four evangelists, symbolic figures of whom were often placed at the four corners in the supports of the vaulting. This part of the church celebrates the God of the Ascension and from it rise the prayers of the congregation towards the heights, where a cupola presents a circular image of celestial perfection.

Lastly, the edifice conveys ideas of the divine order of the cosmos in all its parts, notably in the numerical relations between them which determine their proportions. In monastery schools arithmetic was placed on an equal footing with the science of music. But it was also regarded as an instrument of divination. For according to an ancient tradition each number had an esoteric import knowledge of which was essential for an understanding of the divine plan. For the initiated, in other words the clergy, four was the number of the world, five that of man, and the numeral ten, sum of all the numbers (described by Pythagoras as an expression of the perfect) was the sign of God. Both the most complex monastic basilicas, as at Tournus and Saint-Benoît-sur-Loire, and the simplest churches of the country priories, as at Chapaize and Barberá, conformed to a mathematical schema. For their builders wished them to be, like Gregorian chants, meaningful representations of the harmony of the spheres. To this "scientific" planning they owe that perfect balance which delights us today, but whose hidden meaning we are now unable to decipher.

Of the monk Gunzo who planned the great church of Cluny, we are told that he was "an admirable precentor." And it is clear that in designing this church he had recourse to structural methods resembling those used by the polyphonists of a later age for the composition of motets and fugues. Using as his module a unit measuring five Roman feet, he built up an intricate system of arithmetical relations. Implicit in these numerical values were a host of symbols, charged with other-worldly intimations. The proportions of the apse were based on the number seven; those of the great porch on the progression one, three, nine, twenty-seven. Much importance was assigned to the "perfect numbers" of Isidore of Seville and to the Pythagorean theory of harmonic numbers—an eminently musical conception, appropriate to the order of the universe, mirrored in the balanced structure of the edifice. This network of numerical relations was intended to enwrap the mind and draw it nearer God. For the abbey was dedicated to Peter, fisher of men, and Abbot Hugh of Cluny saw his church as a great net spread out for catching souls.

CHURCH OF SANT'ANGELO IN FORMIS, NEAR CAPUA: VIEW OF THE INTERIOR. LAST QUARTER OF THE 11TH CENTURY.

CHURCH OF SANTA MARIA IN COSMEDIN, ROME: VIEW OF THE INTERIOR. 11TH AND EARLY 12TH CENTURY.

CHURCH OF SAINT-MARTIN AT CHAPAIZE IN BURGUNDY. BEFORE 1020.

CHURCH OF SANTA MARIA AT BARBERÁ, NEAR BARCELONA. LATE 11TH OR EARLY 12TH CENTURY.

CHURCH OF SAINT-PHILIBERT AT TOURNUS, BURGUNDY: THE NARTHEX. 11TH CENTURY.

CHURCH OF SAINT-PHILIBERT AT TOURNUS, BURGUNDY: GROUND FLOOR OF THE NARTHEX. 11TH CENTURY.

were hewn and fitted together to build the House of God, but by workmen whose wages had to be paid. Chroniclers sometimes attribute the rebuilding of a church to the chance discovery, as if by miracle, of a buried treasure. Bishop Arnoul of Orléans wished his new church to be built with the utmost speed. "One day when the workmen were making soundings, in search of solid ground for the foundations of the new basilica, they discovered a large amount of gold." They handed it over to the bishop and it was said that an earlier prelate, when building the original cathedral, had laid by this hidden reserve to provide for future renovations. Actually that gold came from the cathedral treasury. Many religious communities were then capitalizing on the valuables so long stored away in their treasuries, and also turning to account the precious metals made over to them by Western knights fresh from their campaigns on the confines of Islam. The wealth swallowed up in the building operations at Cluny was enormous. Behind the masterpieces of Romanesque art lay the first economic upsurge of the new Europe in the making.

The chief innovation in the architecture that flourished in southern Gaul, in the area where triumphant feudalism had swept away the Carolingian aesthetic, was a systematic use of vaulting. Architects of the previous age had on occasion resorted to vaulting, using it to roof those parts of the church which, from the eighth century on, had been added to the Frankish basilicas as a result of the development of the liturgy and the cult of relics. The entrance porch and the chevet had accordingly become two-storey units, with large ceremonies taking place on the upper floor. It had thus been necessary, in the crypt and the entrance of the church, to substitute pillars for columns and vaulting for timber-work. The nave, however, remained timber-roofed throughout the eleventh century in all regions where the imperial tradition had maintained itself: Germania, Lorraine, the Ile-de-France, Norman Neustria, and even Italy. It was probably in the smaller monasteries in the mountains of Catalonia that the vaulting was first extended to cover the entire church. This was a significant innovation, made in a province strongly

MARSEILLES, DOME OF THE FORMER CATHEDRAL OF LA MAJOR.

ENNEZAT (AUVERGNE), NAVE AND SOUTH AISLE OF THE CHURCH. LATE 11TH CENTURY.

5

VAULTING

Eleventh-century churches are remarkable for the variety of their design. The men who built them were free to adopt the forms of their choosing. These men were the prelates themselves, like Bernward of Hildesheim, or Hervé of Saint-Martin de Tours who, "filled with the idea of God, set out to rebuild from top to bottom the church in his keeping, making it vaster and higher; under the inspiration of the Holy Spirit, he showed the workmen where to lay the foundations of this admirable edifice which he himself brought to completion just as he had planned it." Neither the abbots nor the bishops knew anything of architectural theory. They worked empirically, trying to reproduce the forms of some building they had admired, or copying from memory some other which had close ties with their own church. The art of church-building thus progressed by a series of random experiments until the ground had been prepared for the magnificent achievements of around 1100.

This progress, whose results were noticed and commented on by Rudolph Glaber, was made possible by the economic expansion which, around 1000, was beginning to raise Europe from the slough of poverty and barbarism. For these walls were erected by whole armies of salaried quarrymen, carters, stonecutters and masons. It was not by forced labor or volunteers that these mighty stones

CARDONA (NEAR BARCELONA), DOME OF THE COLLEGIATE CHURCH OF SAN VICENTE. CONSECRATED IN 1040.

PÉRIGUEUX, CATHEDRAL OF SAINT-FRONT, DOME OF THE MAIN BELL-TOWER. 1125-1150.

influenced by Mozarabic culture and invigorated, round about 1000, by thriving trade. The abbots of Cuxa, Canigou and Ripoll were enlightened, open-minded men. They were well versed in mathematics and, in Spain, well placed to benefit by the advances made in building techniques by Islamic architects. The methods they experimented with were carried northwards along the trade routes and pilgrim roads into Provence and the Toulouse area, from there to Tours, then into Burgundy and so to Cluny, which diffused them far and wide.

The new, vaulted nave at Vézelay was erected about 1135 to replace a timber roof destroyed by fire. The churchmen who created the Romanesque aesthetic had, however, higher aims in view than merely fireproofing the House of God. That was but an incidental advantage of their immense and arduous venture, their persevering efforts in the face of mishaps and setbacks to throw a barrel vault across the main nave, to absorb the thrust by groined arches in the side aisles, to extend the galleries, to stabilize the domes. For vaulting was one of the cardinal elements of the architectural style created by the medieval churchmen—a style which they intended to be an expression of the visible and invisible worlds, and a means of uplifting man to an apprehension of transcendental realities. Possibly too, at a time when the monastic Church was enlarging its funerary functions and thus coming into favor with the mass of laymen, the Benedictine abbots may have aimed at shrouding the whole church in that dim religious light of crypt and vestibule in which the burial rites, prelude of a glorious resurrection, could be most tellingly celebrated. It is certainly true that by the substitution of a stone for a wooden roof the church gained a unity of atmosphere which made it an apter symbol of the One World created by the divine will. Vaulting, moreover, greatly improved the acoustics of a building whose primary function consisted largely in vocal and musical ceremonies. Finally, and above all, vaulting introduced the circle into the architectural rhythms—an image of the cycle of Time, a perfect, never-ending line, the clearest symbol of Eternity and of that heavenly reward to which the monastic church sped the shriven believer on the day of his death.

IV

QUEST OF THE INVISIBLE

LITURGY

In the eleventh century the monks of Europe made their way to God by two distinct routes. One group kept to the trail blazed long before by Byzantine Christendom and the axis of its greatest successes lay along the neutral zone spanning central Italy and dividing Latinism from Hellenism. Needless to say its sphere of influence was not limited to this narrow area; it extended into Sicily and the tip of the peninsula, which Norman lords were gradually conquering at the expense of both Byzantium and Islam, annexing it to the West, and where they soon built (in Bari) a Romanesque cathedral. In these lands the monk truly withdrew from the world and made his abode in the wilderness. In Sinai and in Cappadocia he lived in solitary squalor in a cavern, naked, covered with vermin, treating his body with scorn and living on what God in His goodness accords to the lilies of the field and the birds of the air. The mountains of Latium, Tuscany and Calabria teemed with anchorites and there were many little groups of hermitages where, under the guidance of a master, a band of disciples mortified their flesh for the salvation of their souls. As time went on, these colonies of solitaries joined forces in organized communities such as the Order of Camaldolesi founded by St Romuald. Not only Italians adopted this sternly penitential way of life. The emperor Otto III betook himself to St Nilus, another champion of mortification; accompanied by Francon, Bishop of Worms, "he made his way in the utmost secrecy, barefoot and wearing a hair-shirt, to a cave near the Church of Christ, and there they abode fourteen days, fasting, keeping vigil and saying prayers." This style of monastic life, involving a renunciation of the world, total poverty, seclusion in a cell and silence, ruled out any artistic activity —except when, as for instance at Pomposa, the foundation was a worldly success. One of the reasons why in the eleventh century the prestige of the monasteries steadily increased was doubtless its appeal to the knighthood who could appreciate the physical heroism, the feats of endurance, required of

the monks. Monachism proliferated everywhere; it took root in the heart of the West when St Bruno founded the Grande Chartreuse, and St Stephen of Muret the Order of Grandmont. To it was due the tinge of austerity which began to invade the Romanesque aesthetic and prepared the way for the technical and visual achievements of Cistercian art. But its real triumph came after 1140. During the period we are here concerned with western monasticism for the most part took another path, the one that St Benedict of Nursia had traced in the sixth century. Diffused from Monte Cassino, from the abbey of Saint-Benoît-sur-Loire (which claimed to possess the relics of the founder) and above all by England which had been evangelized by the Order, the Rule of St Benedict had been imposed by the Carolingian reformers on all the monasteries of Europe.

The new Benedictine way approximated to the earlier one since it, too, called for abstinence and reclusion and dispensed with missionary activities. But it differed from its predecessor in two respects; it instilled moderation and the spirit of confraternity. Each Benedictine monastery housed a community resembling a family firmly governed by a "father," the abbot, having all the powers and responsibilities of the paterfamilias in ancient Rome. All were brothers and the laws prohibiting any individual monk from acting independently were even stricter than those of the consanguinity binding together children of the same father. St Benedict stressed the monastic virtue of obedience. "Prompt and positive obedience," he said, "is the first step in our practice of humility. Renounce your own will and gird on the noble and potent weapon of obedience for your battles under the banner of Christ, our true King." Weapons, battles, a banner—the community of monks was envisaged as an army pledged to obey the orders of a military commander. They could indeed be described as enlisted men, for all of them had to sign a written undertaking like the one signed by soldiers of the Late Empire. They practised the team spirit in the fullest sense and none had a moment's solitude, not even the abbot of the monastery. He took his meals, slept and prayed among his "sons" and comrades, and the bond between them was far closer, even more irrevocable, than that between the vassal and his lord.

Among the other cardinal virtues in the Benedictine ethic was stability, there was no longer any question of wandering from place to place and the monk spent all his life in the monastery of his profession. Like the feudal families, the community established itself permanently in a domain which supplied it with the necessaries of life. None of its members owned any private property and each could honestly describe himself as poor. But in point of fact his poverty differed little from that of a knight's son who, though his father might be wealthy, had no resources of his own. And it was even more like that of the "domestic" warriors incorporated in the households of the greater lords: men whose weapons were their only personal possession. For like the common soldier, the monk participated in a collective source of wealth which provided him with his sustenance and with the rough-and-ready but substantial amenities then enjoyed by the rural nobility. Since it had so many of the characteristics of the establishments of the feudal lords, the Benedictine monastery fitted quite readily into the culture-pattern of the early Middle Ages and could welcome within its walls both young scions of the nobility and ageing knights anxious to spend their last days in a place dedicated to God's service. This was all the more understandable since the monastery was pervaded by the spirit of moderation inculcated by St Benedict's precepts: the habit of a well-tempered life, discretion, a sense of measure and a sound commonsense—the qualities to which this "little Rule for the beginner" owed its success. "We trust we are not enjoining anything onerous or over-stringent." For St Benedict disapproved of extreme asceticism; he limited the periods of fasting and, discouraging indulgence in mysticism, advocated a simple, forthright morality. To his mind, Christ's soldiers, if they were to win the day, should be allowed proper clothes, sufficient food, a reasonable amount of sleep. The monk, he held, did better to forget his body than persist in fighting it down; let him cultivate to good effect the land around his House so as to wean from it more copious harvests and offer to God more abundant sacrifices.

Cluny kept to the Benedictine Rule, but interpreted it in its own way, and from the inflexions that the Cluniac *consuetudines* gave the master's teaching derived undoubtedly some of the basic characteristics of the Romanesque aesthetic. From the start the Cluniac Order occupied that place in the hierarchy which from the earliest period of Latin Christendom had been assigned to God's servants: the highest rung of the social ladder. It felt no qualms about utilizing the great wealth that accrued from the steady flow of alms into each of its Houses. For the abbots felt sure that by no other hands could that wealth be expended on a worthier purpose. Did not the Order devote these alms wholly to the service of God? Why, then, refuse them? And since the Order of Cluny constituted as it were an earthly vanguard of the hosts of heaven, surely her sons, like the knights, were justified in "living like lords" and being supported by the labors of the peasantry which, by God's will, provided both fighting men and monks with their sustenance. St Benedict had wished the monks to be self-supporting, to till their fields and reap their harvests. Cluny, however, surrendered to the spirit of the nobility who thought it quite natural for free men to lead a leisured life, and regarded manual labor as dishonorable and degrading, of the nature of a punishment; surely it was God's will that some men should be slaves. So the monks of Cluny performed only symbolic tasks and, like the nobles, were served by tenants cultivating their domains and left all menial duties to a staff of domestics. Though men of leisure, the monks were not men of learning. St Benedict took no interest in intellectual pursuits, he was concerned with men's souls, not with their minds, and in terms of his Rule quite illiterate persons had an equal right with the best educated of entry to the monastery. The Anglo-Saxon Benedictines, however, whose recommendation inspired the reform that took place in the eighth century had thought differently and seen in the abbey school a mainstay of the monastic life, and, Latin being to them an unknown tongue, they made a point of studying it, even reading Virgil. This is why the Germanic and Gallic monasteries had developed into flourishing centers of culture in the Carolingian period. In 1000 many such still existed in the lands most deeply marked by the imperial imprint: Bavaria, Swabia, Catalonia. The best libraries, the ablest teachers of the eleventh century were to be found at St Gall and Reichenau, at Monte Cassino, Bec and Ripoll. But not at Cluny.

For a movement against all intellectual pursuits was in progress in the Cluny congregation, a movement that had begun in certain abbeys of the Empire on the eve of the ninth century. It had not gone to the point of closing the school or locking up the bookcases, but there was a tendency to reduce the mental pabulum of the monks to readings from the Fathers, particularly St Gregory the Great. After 1000, Cluniac abbots did their best to discourage studies of the pagan classics and warned their monks of the spiritual danger incurred by surrendering to the charms of Latin poetry. The fact that this mistrust of the *auctores* of Classical Antiquity prevailed in the circles in which the Romanesque aesthetic took its rise helps us to understand why it differed so markedly from the imperial aesthetic and from all the "renaissances" motivated by a will to humanism. Of the three subjects of the Trivium the monk confined himself to the third, the art of grammar. What use could Rhetoric be to a man who seldom spoke and usually expressed himself by gestures? Equally useless was Dialectic, weapon of argument; in the cloister there was no occasion for discussing or persuading. So only grammar remained. But that was no justification for exposing the monk to the lures of pagan literature. He could learn the meaning of Latin words quite well enough from textbooks such as the *Etymologiae* of Isidore of Seville. With the aid of reference books of this kind, in which the gist of the great works of the past was set forth in a matter-of-fact manner stripped of any pernicious "glamour," the sons of St Benedict could peruse in the seclusion of the cloister a few sacred texts and gradually memorize them. For surely it was not by dint of reasoning, still less by a surrender to the magic of fine writing, that the Christian could acquire the true knowledge needful for his spiritual well-being. The monk had dedicated himself to silence and a long pilgrimage towards the light divine. He would obtain that ultimate enlightenment more speedily if he gave free play to remembered words and images, welling up unsummoned from the depths of consciousness; flashes of intuition would leap forth from associations of these words and from the symbols they evoked. Such was the mental climate in which the sacred painting, sculpture and architecture of the eleventh century came to florescence. There was no question here of logic or method, and allusions to the classical writers were few and far between. The one thing needful was a full and faithful memory of Holy Writ, each word

being regarded as a God-given sign and therefore treasured, pondered on, turned over in the mind, manipulated, until a chance contact with another term struck out a sudden, new illumination. A train of thought, illogical in substance, a compound of vagrant reminiscences, it none the less became coherent in the ordered symbolism of the liturgy.

For basic to the Cluniac way of monastic life was its convergence on the great act of service, the *opus Dei* (as St Benedict called it): the public celebration of the canonical office. All the modifications made by the *ordo cluniensis* combined to elaborate and multiply these services. St Benedict had already treated communal worship as an essential function of the monastery; it was, he said, the "specific vocation" of the monks to hymn the praises of God, and twelve of the chapters of his Rule dealt with the Administration of the Rites and Ceremonies of the Church. What indeed, he asked, was the purpose of the monastic life if not collective prayer and supplication for the spiritual welfare of Christendom at large? When a school was included in the monastery its only object was to train men for this service, a service best performed by those who had accepted wholeheartedly the vocation of obedience and humility. In it the sense of a collective life—the team spirit, as we now would call it—was intensified by the liturgy into which were interwoven all the flowers of thought and speech the monks had culled from their daily reading and solitary meditations. But in this respect Cluny asked far more of the monks than had the founder of the Order. To begin with, by prolonging the duration of the services. The monks were expected to devote as much time every week to the recitation of the Psalms and to the intoning of passages from sacred texts as to all other occupations. So it was that in the Cluniac *consuetudines* divine service lasted seven hours on ordinary days and still longer on special occasions. To chant continuously for so many hours was physically exhausting; hence the abandonment of manual labor and the relatively comfortable way of life adopted by the Order. Cluny, moreover, made a point of diverting to church ceremonies, for the greater glory of God, the taste for luxury and rich adornment characteristic of the age of chivalry. What was to be done with all the wealth that was pouring in from the great estates in an ever-increasing flow now that they were better managed, and much of which all good Christians, as in duty bound, were making over to the abbey: the pieces of gold, ingots of silver that the knights of Christ, vanquishers of Islam, were constantly donating to the great monastery? Surely they could not be better employed than for enhancing the splendor of its ceremonies. So it was that the Cluniac monasteries combined to form as it were one gigantic workshop in which all who had any skill in the arts devoted their talents to adorning the House of God. Rudolph Glaber had this in mind when he spoke of "the friendly rivalry which led each community to seek to have a church more beautiful than those of its neighbors" and caused the world "to shake itself, cast off its ancient garment and clothe itself everywhere with a white robe of churches." But these edifices, their lavish decorations and the profusion of goldsmiths' work around the altars were only the outer husk, a tegument perfectly adjusted to contain it, of a work of art far vaster than they and renewed day after day in the elaborate ritual of the Cluniac liturgy.

Throughout the year these rites enacted a sort of ballet in very slow motion, miming man's lot on earth, his destiny and the march of Time from the Creation to the Last Day. The physical participation of the community of monks in this celebration of the divine plan began with a procession, signifying the progress of God's people led by Moses to the Promised Land; thereafter by Christ to the heavenly Jerusalem. In the Carolingian period this fundamental rite had determined the layout of the new abbatial foundations. At Saint-Riquier, for example, three separate churches were built at some distance from each other and in the course of the procession the monks visited each in turn, and by an instinctive response to a symbolic analogy the thoughts of all were drawn to another triad, that of the Persons of the Trinity. Similarly, the exigences of the processional liturgy determined the structure of the Romanesque basilicas; new side aisles were added to the central nave, and these were prolonged by an ambulatory circling the choir, frequent openings being provided at appropriate points. The growing tendency to increase the length of the church was due to the same cause. In the third church at Cluny St Hugh, its builder, with a view to suggesting more emphatically the long road man must follow to attain salvation, arranged for a wide gap between the entrance, place of initiation into the divine light, and the central point where the sacrifice was solemnized and where the monks' collective prayers rose towards God—the part of the church where the soaring movement was intensified by the upward thrust of columns and vaults: the choir.

The liturgic act was, first and foremost, musical; the spiritual fervor of the eleventh century found its most complete expression in chants sung in unison by a male choir. They voiced that unanimity which pleased God in the praises of His creatures. Seven times daily the monks made a processional entrance into the church to sing the Psalms and the "psalm-tones" used by them had the distinctive qualities of Benedictine plain chant as opposed to that of Oriental monachism: restraint, decorum, an interpretation ruling out any touch of individual fantasy. For at Cluny the practice of humility and obedience applied equally to the precentor to whom the abbot had delegated his functions of training, conducting and leading the choir. We must not assume, however, that originality was completely excluded in the monasteries of the West. Several great eleventh-century abbeys, such as St Gall and Saint-Martial of Limoges, took an active part in developing the major art of the age, liturgic art, and devising new, happier associations of words and melodies. In the technical language of the day the verb *trouver* ("finding") meant just this: arranging and adapting new texts to the modulations of the plain song. The men who specialized in this fully realized that in so doing they were often bound to modify—for a religious end—the accepted grammar. This called for much ingenuity, since it was no easy task wedding the vocabulary of prayer to the vast, simple rhythms of Gregorian melodies, perfectly adjusted to those of the cosmos, *ergo* to the divine mind. No easy task, but a noble one, for were they not sublimating forms of human speech to those of the hymns of praise chanted forever by the angels? In eleventh-century schools the Quadrivium, second cycle of the liberal arts, consisted almost entirely of music and to this the other subjects—arithmetic, geometry, astronomy—were subordinated. By common consent the art of music was the climactic point of the grammatical studies composing the Trivium. Since no one read in a speaking voice, since all public reading was vocalized in the manner of a recitative, and since, if it was to be faultless, the singing of the psalms called both for a knowledge by rote of the sacred text and an understanding of its meaning, the study of Latin vocables and that of musical sounds marched side by side. In this culture the logic of musical consonances ranked as the only perfect logic. When Gerbert proposed "to make fully perceptible the various notes by marking them off on the monochord, dividing their consonances and symphonies by tones, half-tones and sharps, and distributing them according to the intervals of the scale," he was anticipating the scholastic analysis of sounds made two centuries later. But what most of all he hoped for was to gain thereby an insight into the underlying order of the universe.

Music and, through it, the liturgy were undoubtedly the most potent instruments of knowledge known to eleventh-century culture. By reason of their symbolical significance and the mental associations evoked by them, the words of the liturgy enabled the Christian to plumb the mysteries of the cosmos; they led him towards God. And music led to Him more directly still, since it revealed the transcendent harmonies of the created world and by its instant action on the human heart led man to participate, indeed to merge himself, in the perfection of the divine plan. In Chapter xx of his Rule St Benedict had quoted a line from the Psalms "I shall sing to thee in the presence of the angels." In the choir of monks he saw a prefiguration of the choirs of heaven; overleaping the barriers between this world and the next, it gave the earthbound mortal access to the supernal realm and to the uncreated Light. "When we join our voices in these chants," St Benedict had said, "we stand in the very presence of God and His angels." For then the whole man—body, soul and spirit—is flooded by that divine illumination; he attains the *stupor* and the *admiratio* told of by the twelfth-century mystic Baldwin of Ford, and is rapt in contemplation of the eternal splendor. Monasticism made no attempt to rationalize its faith; rather, to stimulate it by the collective emotion of the congregations in the daylong services. Unconcerned with causes and effects or logical demonstration, it entered into communication with the unseen powers, the most

direct avenue to which was the choral singing of the liturgy. When week by week, at the same hour, the monk sang the same verses to the same melodies, did he not by the very act of joining in the plain song participate in depth in an experience of the ineffable, unattainable by any other means? "The rites which, as prescribed in the Calendar for the Year, take place in the divine service are signs of the highest realities, contain the holiest sacraments and all the majesty of the celestial mysteries. They were ordained for the glory of Our Lord Jesus Christ, Head of the Church, by men who understood the sublimity of the aforesaid mysteries and made it known by spoken words, by writings and by rites. Among the many spiritual treasures with which the Holy Spirit has enriched his Church, we should cultivate devoutly that one which aids to an understanding of what we say in prayers and chants." And Rupert of Deutz adds: "This is nothing short of a manner of prophesying."

In the social order of the eleventh century the monks were ministrants of a ceremony of constant praises of the Lord, a rite invested with all the creative powers of a work of art. Thus this work, closely connected with the liturgy, was even more intimately bound up with the art of music. St Hugh of Cluny thought fit to install in the center of the new basilica, on the capitals of the choir, a representation of all the tones of music since, for him, they equated a cosmogony in virtue of those occult correspondences which, according to Boethius, linked the seven notes of the scale to the seven planets and gave a key to the harmony of the spheres. But it was most of all as a sort of diagram of the divine mystery that the abbot proposed them to the contemplation of the monks. *Tertius impigit Cristumque resurgens fingit*; in this inscription beside the figure was defined the function of the third tone. By the emotion it arouses it enables the soul, better than any words or imagery could do, to sense the true significance of the Resurrection of Our Lord.

Very few could read. For the great majority speech and gestures were the only means of communication. Each time he uttered certain words of power a man established contact with the mysterious world around him. There were formulas of exorcism which expelled evil spirits from possessed persons; of oaths calling God to witness to a compact entered into; of anathema bringing down divine reprisals on the head of an offender; of the sacraments which opened the doors of heaven to the believer. If the prayers chanted by the assembled monks had such efficacy, this was because they were a collective invocation. While they rose heavenwards the barriers between God and mortal man fell one after another—like the walls of Jericho. The word, then, triumphed over the invisible; captured it; enlisted its powers and bent it to its use.

God Himself spoke through His prophets; His utterances are enshrined in the Scriptures and man has no better weapon in his fight against evil than the words recorded there. Dark words in many cases, and the aims of all the teaching in the monastery and the cathedral schools was to make their meaning clear. The churchmen tried to do this by collating the vocables employed in the Scriptures and seeking to detect the occult links between them. "To elucidate a word by means of another word," was the function assigned to the gloss by Conrad of Hirsau. These words were inscribed in the phylacteries which, carved in stone or ivory, were upheld by prophets and apostles. Painters and sculptors, too, used these texts, for their chief task in the eleventh century was to illustrate the Word of God.

In or about 810 Charlemagne had founded, above a martyry and a graveyard, the monastery of Saint-Savin. The church was built in the second quarter of the eleventh century, then adorned with frescoes. Each part of the edifice was given images appropriate to its religious functions, those of the life of the patron saint being placed in the crypt (where the relics were housed) and those of the Apocalypse in the porch. A long barrel vault in the nave provided a large space for painting, uninterrupted by ceiling beams and here the tale of mankind, as recorded in Genesis, from the Creation till the time of Moses, up to the giving of the Law, was represented. The history of the race, as here depicted, revealed the divine plan governing the lot of individual man and heralded the coming of the Messiah and Christ's return on the Last Day. The narrative comprises thirty-six scenes in which earth colors, white and yellow ochres, predominate. But the semicircle of the vault, like the canopy of heaven, enframing the successive episodes, translates them into the world eternal.

ABBEY CHURCH OF SAINT-SAVIN-SUR-GARTEMPE, POITOU: VIEW OF THE NAVE WITH CEILING FRESCOES. 11TH CENTURY.

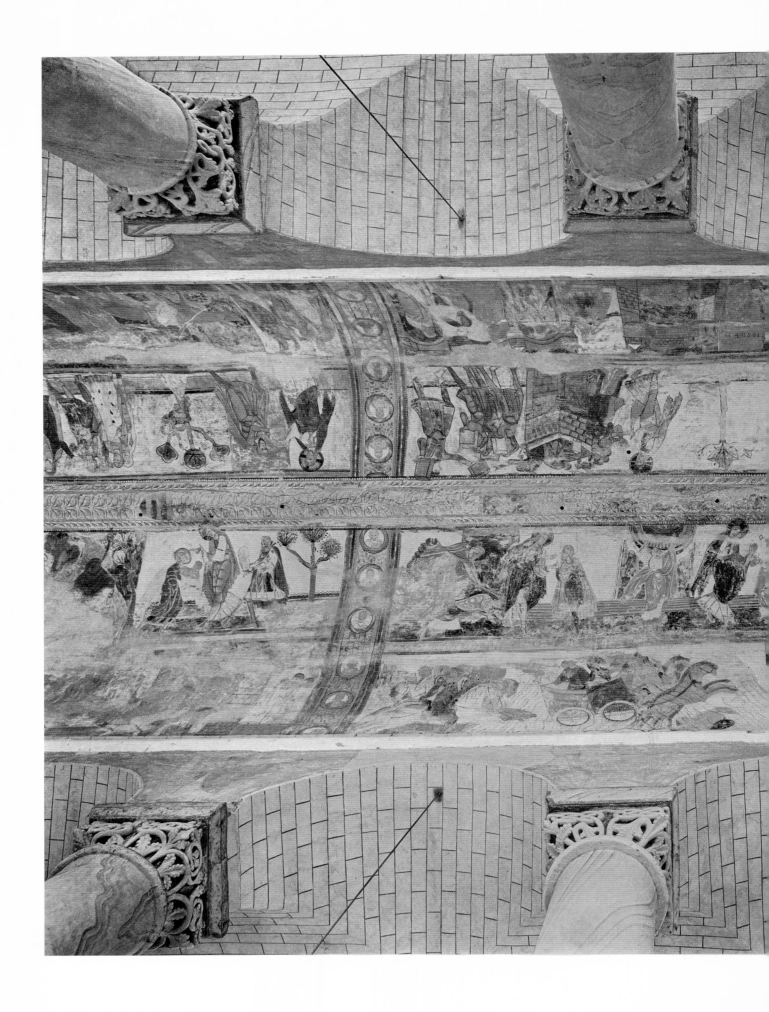

SCENES FROM THE OLD TESTAMENT. 11TH
CENTURY. FRESCOES ON THE VAULT OF THE
NAVE, ABBEY CHURCH OF SAINT-SAVIN-SUR-
GARTEMPE, POITOU.

163

THE PROPHET ISAIAH. ABOUT 1130.
SCULPTURE FROM THE PORTAL OF THE ABBEY CHURCH OF SOUILLAC, PÉRIGORD.

ST PETER AND ST PAUL. ABOUT 1120-1150. DOOR-JAMB OF THE NARTHEX.
CHURCH OF THE MADELEINE, VÉZELAY, BURGUNDY.

MASTER OF ECHTERNACH (?). ST PAUL. ABOUT 1000. IVORY BOOK-COVER. MUSÉE DE CLUNY, PARIS.

In the Old Testament God speaks through the mouths of the prophets; in the Gospels He speaks in person. Jesus, the Word incarnate, delivers His message directly. It was the duty of every monk, if he wished to follow Christ and to identify himself with the disciples who heard the Master speaking in the hills of Galilee, to make himself familiar with the sacred text, "full of true words and wonders"—to hearken to it, read it or, best of all, copy it with his own hand.

To write down the words of God, to shape each letter slowly, like a graver, on that stubborn material, parchment—an exacting task that Peter the Venerable likened to the ploughman's toil ("in each furrow you trace on the page sow the good seed of God's word")—this was, like the discipline of the liturgical plain song, to dedicate one's labors to God. The work done in the scriptorium ranked among the practices of monastic asceticism. For like prayer and fasting, Abbon of Fleury pointed out, it helps to drive away evil thoughts, to escape the thrall of the flesh and to open the mind to higher things. Since they were receptacles of the word of God, these books were given the aspect of a shrine, were lavishly adorned, bound in finely wrought leather or in gold, and made resplendent, like the sides of reliquaries, with carved ivories and precious stones. For the same reason illuminations supplement the text in the transmission of the divine message. Indeed the making of each book was regarded as an act of consecration. The two monks at Stavelot who in the eleventh century copied a text by Josephus, employed the same formula that the priest used in the dedication of the Host. "Receive, Holy Trinity, the offering of this book." Both the readers of the book and those who were to preserve it till the end of time participated in this offering and in its talismanic virtues. For, like relics, like even the Holy Sacrament, these objects in which words and images were combined were regarded as intermediaries to which men could resort with a view to obtaining God's favor and a passport to eternity. No distinction, in fact, was drawn between the making of a book, in which the patience of the scribe, the commentator's learning and the talent of the painter co-operated, and an act of thanksgiving. When the Germanic emperors commissioned, at Reichenau or Echternach, a Gospel Book or a Book of Pericopes; when Henry III presented to Speyer Cathedral the Codex Aureus, *they were not so much thinking of adding to their glory by an act of high munificence, as conscious of "officiating." They were fulfilling the sacred, priestlike function enjoined by the state to which God had called them.*

MASTER OF MONTE CASSINO. THE SONS OF ZEBEDEE. LAST QUARTER OF THE 11TH CENTURY.
FRESCO, CHURCH OF SANT'ANGELO IN FORMIS, NEAR CAPUA.

BOOK OF PERICOPES OF HENRY II: CHRIST TAKING LEAVE OF THE DISCIPLES.
REICHENAU, ABOUT 1010. FOLIO 136 RECTO, CLM. 4452, STAATSBIBLIOTHEK, MUNICH.

MISSEL OF SAINT-DENIS: CHRIST IN MAJESTY. ABOUT 1050.
FOLIO 15 VERSO, MS LAT. 9436, BIBLIOTHÈQUE NATIONALE, PARIS.

in general, and especially manuscript illumination (which seems to have furnished most of the themes used in large-scale monumental decoration), was strongly influenced by the arts of the goldsmith and the jeweler which, well represented in the church treasure, preserved the traditions of the art of classical Antiquity. Even when it decorated a wall, painting remained closely related to a text, which its purpose was to illustrate. Of each word, each verse, each paragraph, it gave a visual equivalent which, like the glosses of the school, helped to elucidate and clarify the text. The painter used quite simple images, very close to what the eye perceives; all he did was to record the normal data of perception and fit them into an ordered pattern.

Still, some of the texts he illustrated relate to signs and wonders and here the artist could exercise his imagination, indulge in fantastic visions, notably when his themes were taken from the Book of Revelation. The Gospels, on the other hand, tell of everyday things and people, of inns and robbers, of kings following a star, of caves and fishermen, figtrees, lances, thorns, a storm-tossed lake. Doubtless the narrative contains references to the world invisible, but these are relatively rare; almost all the action takes place on earth, among human beings. This explains why the life of Jesus has so small a place in eleventh-century iconography. To men who saw the world around them as a prison and were always groping to find a fissure in its walls, an escape from the perils and privations of daily life, and who tried to forget their present afflictions by dreaming of a splendid Hereafter, the text of the synoptic Gospels may well have seemed too drab and colorless. They wanted to be told of the glories to come, not reminded of present hardships. For their priests and monks, too, what counted was not the story of Christ's humble life on earth, but visions of the Eternal Life.

None the less, readings from the Gospels formed part of the liturgy and these texts were illustrated. Pictures of Christ preaching, His miracle of the loaves and fishes, His triumph over the temptations of the devil and His converse with the disciples bulk large in the pages of illuminated manuscripts, Gospel Books or Books of Pericopes in which passages from

THE PRESENTATION IN THE TEMPLE. ABOUT 1120. BAS-RELIEF IN THE SOUTH TRANSEPT.
CHURCH OF SAINTE-CROIX, LA CHARITÉ-SUR-LOIRE.

EPISODES OF THE DEATH
OF JOHN THE BAPTIST. 12TH CENTURY.
CAPITAL FROM THE FORMER CLOISTER
OF SAINT-ETIENNE, TOULOUSE.
MUSÉE DES AUGUSTINS, TOULOUSE.

THE KISS OF JUDAS
AND THE ARREST OF CHRIST.
12TH CENTURY. CAPITAL FROM THE
CLOISTER OF LA DAURADE, TOULOUSE.
MUSÉE DES AUGUSTINS, TOULOUSE.

6

THE LIFE OF JESUS

The art and culture of the eleventh century were rooted in a dark forest of primitive beliefs. It was taken for granted that only by magical operations, by incantations and sorcery, could man free himself from the grip of the unseen, elemental forces lurking behind the veil of appearances. The cult of relics, the sacramental rites and the liturgy belonged to the same non-rational universe as amulets and wizardry. They operated in the same manner, had the same purpose: that of bending the sacred to a human will. The work of art had a like function; it explored the unknowable, it provided clues through the labyrinth of the spiritual world and attempted to lift the veils, one by one. Like the churchmen, the medieval artist aimed at clarifying two great mysteries: the realm of nature and the text of Holy Scripture.

The architect's commentary on them is cast in an abstract form. He does not speak in images properly so called, but by signs less easily grasped, by the arrangement and harmony of masses, and by a mathematical formula implicit in the overall structure of the edifice. He formulates a complex of symbols which act imperceptibly on the minds and souls of those who live and pray in the ordered space which he creates. The painter, obviously, keeps closer to visual reality, he depicts, and, unlike the architect's, his language is that of allegory. Painting the New Testament were collated for use at divine service. Scenes of Christ's childhood and Passion adorned the capitals of certain cloisters, intermingled with images symbolizing the powers of evil. They also figure at the top of the long lines of pillars flanking the processions of the monks towards the Light. For each episode of the life of Jesus marks a stage of man's journey to the Last Judgment and his resurrection. Yet during the eleventh century —and this is noteworthy—in none of these images is Jesus represented, as yet, as a brother; always He is the Master, the Lord, the Judge. For most of the monks of Europe the incidents of His life on earth were primarily metaphors of the sacred, signs in the secret vocabulary of man's heavenly guides, symbols he was invited to interpret. For the monks the Gospel narrative described a long ascent at whose summit stood Christ in glory, clad in the splendors of God's kingdom. This is why the painters represented the apostles on the gold grounds of the Pericopes as beings outside Time and the human situation. Who in this age could have pictured as fishermen or paupers St James or St Paul, those all-powerful saints whose tomb was the scene of miracles, who launched thunderbolts and fell diseases on those who belittled their authority. No wonder, then, that Christians of the year 1000 were indisposed to think of the human side of Christ. Romanesque art pictured the apostles as denizens of the invisible world, that of the Lord Jesus who, risen from the dead on Easter Day, forbade the Holy Women to touch Him and returned to heaven in the Ascension: the Pantocrator lording it in the apses of Cluny and Tahull.

Nevertheless it is in these images of the living Son of Man, present in this world, that we find the source of the ideology which was later to make the Gothic cathedral a hymn of praise to the Incarnation. For was not the very act of carving in stone, as in the cloister of Santo Domingo de Silos, the figures of men and women grouped around the dead Christ's body, or St Thomas laying his hand on the wound, tantamount to introducing the divine essence into dead matter and creating a concrete figuration of the mystery that the ablest theologians in Europe were seeking to elucidate?

THE WAY TO EMMAUS. 12TH CENTURY.
BAS-RELIEF ON THE NORTHWEST PILLAR.
CLOISTER OF SANTO DOMINGO DE SILOS, NEAR BURGOS.

THE SUPPER AT EMMAUS.
ABOUT 1080.
IVORY PLAQUE OF AN ALTAR FRONTAL
FROM SALERNO CATHEDRAL.
STAATLICHE MUSEEN, BERLIN.

THE CRUCIFIXION. 12TH CENTURY. BAS-RELIEF ON THE NORTHWEST PILLAR.
CLOISTER OF SANTO DOMINGO DE SILOS, NEAR BURGOS.

THE WORLD ORDER

"God cannot be seen directly. The contemplative life which begins on earth will reach perfection only when God is seen face to face. The meek and simple soul, when, soaring on the wings of speculation and breaking its carnal fetters, it gazes at things celestial, cannot stay long above its terrene self; ineluctably the weight of the flesh drags it back to earth. It is dazzled by the blinding light of heaven, but is soon recalled to itself. Nevertheless the little it has tasted of the divine lovingkindness has greatly refreshed the soul and soon, fired by abounding love, it hastens to resume its flight." In these words John of Fécamp has well described the monastic ideal. By whole-hearted penitence, obedience, humility and a life of brotherly love the monk aspired to break free from the prison-house in which his senses, and his extreme difficulty in subduing them, held eleventh-century man captive. He was engaged in a never-ending struggle to overpass the limits of normal perception and human understanding, to glimpse the splendors of that new world of light which, after the resurrection on the Last Day, will be revealed to all mankind, and even now to gain admittance to that other part of the universe whose stupendous possibilities could be surmised but not perceived as yet. A thirst for God—that is to say for mystery.

For, however learned they might be, the clergy were still unable to intellectualize their faith. Their reasoning powers were in fact as feeble as the wooden ploughshares drawn by half-starved oxen in the farmlands. They could not read Greek and the philosophy of the ancients was, to them, a dead letter. The few scientific treatises bequeathed to them by moribund Rome—a Rome that in any case set little store on intellectual acquirements—did nothing to free their minds of the illogical ways of thinking current among the peasantry. Like the hunters and warriors, their kinsmen, who always felt uneasy when they ventured into strange country or the perils of war, the men of God were constantly on their guard, apprehensive of what might lie in wait

for them. Gerbert, whose culture was so widely admired in the year 1000, had the reputation of being a magician, not a philosopher. He, too, laid snares for the invisible and sought to propitiate the dark powers of fate by spells and ruses. The men of that age had a feeling of being lost in a dark forest. God lurked somewhere in that forest but His presence could be detected only by vague, half-hidden imprints, traces of His handiwork. These made it possible to follow up His trail, and by dint of infinite patience and persistence, not indeed to have sight of Him, but perhaps to catch fleeting gleams of His passing.

The collective rites enabled men, by means of chants and cultic gestures, to share in the mystery of the divine, to quit their earthbound selves, to come in touch with the transcendent and, as Rupert of Deutz put it, themselves to become "prophets," in other words harbingers of God. This is why music and the liturgy ranked highest as a means to grasp the inapprehensible. No one as yet believed this could be done by logic. But exegesis could help, and to this all the mental activities of the time were directed. For from the hidden God came signs, mysterious as Himself, and the first thing needful was to learn to decipher them. Since the revival of education in the Carolingian monasteries all the methods of teaching tended to this end. The Benedictine monk Hrabanus Maurus, *Praeceptor Germaniae* (educator of Germany), who was Abbot of Fulda in the second quarter of the ninth century, was a pioneer in this field. "It occurred to me," he wrote, "to compile a small work dealing not only with the nature of things and the proper usage of words but also with their mystical significance." As things stood, words and nature constituted the two domains accessible to the human mind in which God deigned to manifest Himself. The primary study of the monk was the Scriptures, and the chief function of the teaching of grammar was to train him to make the transition from the textual to the underlying connotation, the mystical significance, of each word. He also scrutinized the created world, searching for the analogies whose unbroken chain could guide him towards enlightenment. "By the manifold differences of figures and forms which the Creator has established between His creatures, He willed that the soul of the man of understanding, by way of what the eyes perceive and the mind apprehends, should attain to a simple knowledge of the divine. For," Glaber continues, "these undeniable relationships between things tell us of God in a silent testimony, at once clear and elegant. There is a continuous progression whereby each thing reveals within itself the other thing; and, after making known the Principle from which it proceeds, tends to revert to its primal entity."

The methodology of the age was based on these assumptions. Since it was God who created the universe perceived by our senses there exists an identity of substance between the Almighty and His creature, or at least some fundamental union, that *universitas* of which John Scotus Erigena spoke. Thus it is possible to discern God by contemplating the world He has made and progressing step by step *per visibilia ad invisibilia*, from things seen to things not seen. The whole creation bears constant witness to the divine purpose and tells us all we need to know. But just as we can arrive at a true understanding of Holy Writ by studying the relations between words, lines and passages in the Old and New Testaments, so a wise study of the infinite diversity of forms and figures in the visible world will lead to the discovery of interrelations, harmonies, an order. For the universe is (as William of Conches and Gero of Reichersberg were later to describe it) "an ordered assemblage of creatures" and, in fact, resembles a *magna citara*, a large zither of many strings. This being so, surely it was natural to see in music a royal road to knowledge, since music depends *par excellence* on a just perception of rhythms and consonances and their orderly arrangement. The science of numbers enjoyed equal favor, since the underlying relations between things, insight into which helped to an understanding of the divine plan, were of an arithmetical order. Hence the high place given the symbolism of numbers in the intellectual disciplines of the age. Glaber, for instance, wrote a long dissertation on "the divine quaternity," the mystic significance of the number four, as exemplified by the Evangelists, the natural

elements, the virtues, man's senses, the rivers of paradise, the ages of the world. Thus "quaternity" not only pointed to correspondences between them but also, in the last analysis, reduced the entire universe to a simple formula, symbolic expression of its quintessential unity.

As for art, its sole function was to give visible form to the harmonic structure of the universe, to set out in their due places a certain number of signs, *semata* of the secret language of the inaccessible, by which expression could be given to facts beyond our ken. In short it transposed into simple forms, easily understandable by Christians still in the early stage of initiation, the fruits of the contemplative life. Art was, in fact, a discourse on God, as were music and the liturgy, both of which closely linked up with it. Like them, it aimed at pruning away the tangled overgrowth of appearances and bringing to light the basic values immanent in nature and in the often perplexing text of the Scriptures. Its task was to reveal the underlying structure of the edifice built by the divine architect at the beginning of Time. With this in mind the artists drew on texts recording the words of God, on the images they evoked and on a schema of numbers measuring and defining the rhythms of the universe. Like music and the liturgy, art had recourse to symbols, to novel juxtapositions of discordant values from whose clash a truth flashed forth, and to the rhythms whereby the world is attuned to the breath of God. In their structure, in the positioning of their parts and in the numerical relations between those parts, as in the images they body forth, all the monuments, the gold- and silverware and carvings acted as visual glosses, commentaries on and elucidations of the Scriptures. Concurrently with the development of polyphony and the beginnings of scholasticism, the art language of the period 980-1140 aimed at providing an intuitive understanding of the numinous "something behind everything." More directly than listening or reading, more profoundly than reasoning, the work of art made it possible to apprehend the substantial reality of the universe and learn something of its meaning.

Thus, like music and the liturgy, the architecture and visual arts of the eleventh century were in the nature of an initiation. This is why their forms made no concessions whatever to popular taste. Not in the least intended to appeal to the masses, they catered for a small, restricted élite, for men who had set foot on the ladder of perfection—that is to say primarily for the monks. None the less it was hoped that works of art could take a share—the same as the early type of stage performance then being tried out by the Benedictines at Saint-Benoît-sur-Loire and at St Martial's at Limoges—in the instruction of the common people. In 1025 it was declared at the Synod of Arras that "with the aid of certain painted images the unlettered can perceive what they are unable to get from writing," and the large monumental figurations provided by the "new art" could be seen, on occasion, by the whole Christian community. It was a forthright way of teaching, and some of the largest groups of Romanesque sculpture figuring on the entrances of abbey churches were obviously meant for the edification of the masses and treated, for this reason, in a manner all could understand. (An example is the tympanum at Conques.) But this didactic function was always marginal to creative art, practically all of which emanated from the monks and like the literary, liturgical and musical creations was with few exceptions intended exclusively for them. True, the monastery did not shut its doors against the public, the monks were hospitable folk and on certain days laymen were allowed to attend the services. But they took no real part in them; like the cloister itself, a place of retreat closed to the public, the monastic aesthetic was likewise a "closed" one, introverted, appropriate to men who, turning their backs on the world and all its vanities, headed the pilgrimage of Christendom towards the truth.

For the universe was not static, but subject to the motion God, the Prime Mover, had imposed, and every venture of the spirit was seen as an advance, a progress onward and upward. This progress was made evident and guided by music and the liturgy; and architecture and sculpture, though of their nature unmoving, were called on to implement it. This universal movement took two forms. Firstly, cyclical; the cosmic rhythms, the courses of the stars, the changes of the seasons, day and night, the birth and rebirth of nature—all moved in their appointed orbits, and these continual recurrences were interpreted as symbols of eternity. But in the act of Creation God had stepped forth from His eternity so as to place man, His creature (and even Himself, in virtue of the Incarnation) in Time, and Time ran straight ahead, like a javelin from the hand that hurls it. Henceforth, all things human, the march of history, individual lives, were given a set direction and the work of art, too, needed to be directed towards a precise point in space, if it was to interpret faithfully the divine plan.

The widespread unrest prevailing in western Europe in this momentous century stimulated the idea of progress, of an advance towards some distant goal. In the code of chivalry the quest of adventure had a leading place; indeed it had become almost an obsession with the younger knights, and it was this that sent them post-haste to the four corners of the known world. The first impression given by a reading of the chronicles of the year 1000 is one of a perpetual departure: of pilgrims flocking to shrines, boatmen speeding to fairs to sell cargoes of wine or colored textiles, hordes of peasants, urged on by a vague hope of better things, setting forth under the lead of some half-crazy fanatic to a promised utopia—soon followed by the crusaders and that strange band of fallen women whom Robert d'Arbrissel, founder (about 1100) of the Order of Fontevrault, mustered and led towards redemption. The monks, however, had vowed to stay in their monasteries and, now that the reform of ecclesiastical mores was taking effect, were rarely be to seen on the roads. Even so, shut up in their cloisters, they applied themselves to studying the movements of the world at large and trying to interpret them.

One of their specific functions was the writing of history. This propensity for chronicling contemporary events and recalling those of the past reflected *inter alia* a desire to maintain a venerable tradition, that of the great prose writers of Antiquity. For the teaching of classical Latin in the cloisters was based on a study of the pagan historians, less attention being given to the poets. Sallust seemed less "unsettling" than Virgil from the Christian viewpoint, and the works of Livy figured in the Lenten readings of the monks of Cluny. But this predilection for historical works (which led to the recopying of those of Gregory of Tours in several scriptoria) accorded with one of the chief concerns of monastic culture. For what, in fact, was history but an "inventory" of the Creation? It presented an image of man, and was not man in the image of God? Orderic Vitalis, himself a Benedictine monk and one of the best historians of the period stressed this point. "We should 'sing' history like a hymn of praise to the Creator and just Ruler of all things." Thus history, "a canticle of glory," was given a place in the elaborate liturgy which was regarded in the monasteries as being both an exemplar of the perfect life and a foretaste of the glories of heaven. Moreover, history helps us to trace within the maze of Time the path that man has followed on his way to salvation, to note successive stages of his progress and to discern its orientation. The panoramic view we get from history makes it easier to choose the surest route and set our course to best advantage. Begun on the day of his creation, man's progress has been continuous, and it will remain so until the end of time. The Holy Bible (and what is the Bible but a book of history, divinely inspired?) represents man's gradual advance towards perfection as falling into three parts or phases. In the first, previous to the Incarnation, he was groping in the dark for enlightenment; then the New Testament opened his eyes to better things. But even so, as compared with what he will be after the Second Coming, man is still in the same "under-developed" state as were the worthies of the Old Covenant vis-à-vis the apostles. Early medieval historians were fond of pointing out that the world was growing old and the end of time drawing near. Eleventh-century man lived in constant expectation and terror of the Day of Judgment on which a wrathful God would soon descend in a blaze of light which would be as it were a final baptism of mankind. Prefigurations, then grace and at last glory—such were the three ages of humanity. To all the men of prayer, and particularly to the monks, placed as they were in the heart of a community racked by apprehensions of the Last Day, befell the duty of pointing out the path to follow and making it smooth. The constant processions in the abbey churches symbolized the march of history seen as an ordered progress timed to the rhythms of eternity. But these processions were charged with even loftier intentions; they mimed the entrance into the Kingdom, into the world invisible. All monastic meditation, all monastic art aspired to solve the mystery, rend the veil and glimpse the pure white light of heaven behind it.

Henceforth it seemed less urgent closely to scrutinize the visible world of nature; what was most needed was to advance beyond it. It was in the Bible, more specifically in certain parts of Holy Writ, that images of truth, intimations of the things to come could be discovered. Since in the year 1000

western man had been living in constant anticipation of the end of the world and, taking guidance from the monks, trying to imagine what was soon to meet his gaze—and since all human history was a record of ephemera counting for next to nothing as against Eternity—the Acts of the Apostles, given their "factual" content, were less closely studied than the Old Testament and the Apocalypse. For the former told of the confidence of the righteous man in the beneficence of God and held out hopes of the coming of the Messiah and the attainment of a Promised Land, after a phase of fears and hopes akin to that through which the world was passing now. As for the Book of Revelation, where find a better image of man's future? Does it not describe "the holy city, new Jerusalem" where the wall "was of pure jasper; and the city was pure gold like unto clear glass... and the city had no need of the sun, neither of the moon to shine in it, for the glory of God did lighten it, and the Lamb is the light thereof." These descriptions of the strange and wonderful city seen by the Apocalyptist were incessantly commented on and illustrated in the cloisters. It was observed that, for all its supramundane splendor, the world St John the Divine saw in his vision did not altogether differ from the visible world—which tended to show that according to the divine plan there existed correspondences between the earthly and the heavenly realms. "As I understand it, that mighty Jerusalem is but a reflection, an aspect of the sublime serenity of God. It is governed by the King of Kings, the Lord reigns over it, and this is why he divides its dwellers into grades. None of its shining gates is panelled with metal, the walls are not of stone, stones as we know them do not enter into its walls. It is built of living stones, and living is the gold that paves the streets, whose sheen is brighter than that of the finest earthly gold. Though built to be the city of the angels, it also welcomes hosts of mortals within its walls; one group of its inhabitants rules it, the other lives and breathes in it." There is, in fact, common ground between the cities of men and the Celestial City.

Therefore, when the heavens roll open, we shall be bewildered, yet not feel quite lost in our new abode. Indeed it is possible for man in his life on earth, helped by what he sees, to picture his existence in the after-life. This was done by all the painters who, in Mozarabic Spain, in Aquitanian monasteries, or for the Ottonian emperors, illustrated the text of the Apocalypse itself and the commentaries on it written by Beatus of Liebana. None of them could have wished for a better stimulus to his creative powers, and none of the monks for a theme more apt to launch them on the "successive soarings heavenwards, winged by the love of God" described by John of Fécamp.

Eleventh-century art interpreted the hopes of men who despaired of ever finding in the world they lived in—a hostile, iron-hearted world—the happiness for which they craved. And since they knew this world was transitory, doomed to pass away (perhaps quite soon), and also because the Church aimed at delivering them from its thrall, the art the age needed was not figural. But neither was it abstract—for the good reason that the two worlds corresponded in essentials, nature was a true reflection of the invisible. So the artist drew inspiration from the forms of nature. But he purified them, stripped them of the grosser elements that would be out of place in the glorious after-life, and tried to find equivalences of the gleams of the transcendent glimpsed in moments of illumination. What he wished to depict was the absolute, an aim that corresponded with the aspirations of the monastic milieu which, indeed, was the source of all the art of the period. For the function of the monastery did not consist solely in offering to God the communal and constant praises which were His due, but also in guiding mankind towards salvation. Thus the monks were expected to take the lead, to precede the rank and file of Christendom in their progress to the Light.

The brotherhood of monks had already broken with the temporal world, was sheltered from it by the cloister, had accomplished half the journey and climbed the mountain-top whence, across the mists, they could see, if dimly as yet, the wonders of the Promised Land. The choir of monks joined forces with the choir of angels and the whole culture, all monastic art, was drawn heavenwards by the love of God.

"Who will give us wings like the wings of a dove, so that we can fly across all the kingdoms of the world and make our way to the courts of heaven? Who will lead us into the city of the Great King, where all that we now read in books and see in a glass darkly shall be made visible to our eyes by the grace of God, in the nearness of God, filling our hearts with joy?" Study perhaps, music and the liturgy assuredly, and with them art would point the way. "Let us, then, lift our hands and hearts towards them [the Blessed], and transcend all the passing shows of earthly life. Let our eyes feast unceasingly on the joys that are promised us and rejoice in all that has been already consummated in the believers who, yesterday, were fighting for Christ and reign with Him today in glory. Let us also rejoice in what has been said to us, infallibly; we shall go to 'the land of the living.'" This lyrical apostrophe penned by an anonymous disciple of John of Fécamp gives an admirable idea of the function then assigned to sacred art. It broke the chains of human bondage and it was on the mystery of God that the portal of the cloister opened.

In the eleventh century sacred art was still attempting to condense the teaching of the Gospels into a few signs serving, like the pillar of fire in the wilderness, to guide God's people to the Promised Land. Some of these figurations are highly complex and reflect the intricate symbolism pervading the teaching of the Doctors of the Church. This applies to one of the compositions painted by a deacon under the supervision of Bishop Bernward of Hildesheim on a Gospel Book, to serve as a commentary on the Gospel of St John. His task was to represent the mystery of the Incarnation and reveal in an image how the Word became flesh; to make plain the conjunction between the eternal and the temporal, nature and supernature, God and man. This is why the scene —like the Ascension in the Limoges Sacramentary which depicts a similar conjunction—is laid out in two registers, one above the other. In the upper one Christ sits in glory, holding two symbols, the Lamb of Redemption and the Book of Life. In the lower we are shown the temporal world. The natural forces, sources of evil but under God's control, are represented in two allegories inspired by classical antiquity: Oceanus riding on Leviathan and the Earth Mother holding in her lap Adam, Eve, the Tree of Knowledge and the Serpent—in other words the personages and setting of the Fall. The irruption of the divine into the affairs of men is signified by five rays striking down through the boundary between the supernal and the terrestrial worlds and alighting on the newborn Babe of Bethlehem. There are few works which illuminate to such remarkable effect the way in which the figural methods of classical art were used to body forth ideas wholly concerned with the world ineffable.

In the apse of San Clemente in Rome and in the tympanum of Jaca Cathedral, the symbolism is much simpler; the Incarnation and God's presence in the created world are conveyed by the sign of the cross. The arms of the cross extend in four directions, in the four dimensions of matter, towards the four winds, the four rivers, the four virtues. The cross seals the universe and sanctifies it. It is also an emblem of the peace God promises to man, of His victory over the turbulence of the age, and in the battle ever raging between Good and Evil. At this time crosses were set up on roads to demarcate the zones around monasteries which served as sanctuaries, and in which acts of violence and pillage were strictly prohibited. The badge worn by the crusaders on their garments proclaimed to all that they were on their way to Golgotha, but it meant more than this. It imprinted on their bodies the mark of the paschal sacrifice, of their alliance with the angelic hosts;

it signified that they belonged to the company of the Blessed and already had an appointed place in the Kingdom of Peace to come on the Last Day. Abbot Odilo of Cluny bade his monks see in the cross a promise of universal salvation, a sign of purification enabling all the human race to follow Christ, their Saviour, into the glory of the celestial realm and by the same token a symbol of the two cardinal virtues of monachism: humility and poverty.

At the close of the tenth century the bishops of Germania—great princes whom the emperor had invested with temporal power over their cities and the surrounding country—united in their person the royal function of administering peace and justice with their pastoral charge. They it was who broke with the tradition of refraining from figuring forth the cross as an instrument of torture. A thousand years after the death of Christ the great wooden crosses erected in the center of the basilicas showed the people, for the first time, not a man wearing a kingly crown, but a suffering victim. The apparition of these crosses marked a turning point in the evolution of religious sensibility in the West. Yet, since Romanesque Europe was expecting at any moment the end of the world and since all the relations of men amongst themselves and with the mysterious powers above were envisaged in terms of hierarchies modeled on those of the feudal system, eleventh-century monks and priests preferred epiphanies of Christ in majesty to effigies of Christ crucified. Theirs was above all the Christ of the Apocalypse.

"Behold, a throne was set in heaven, and one sat on the throne. And he that sat was to look upon like a jasper and a sardine stone: and there was a rainbow round about the throne, in sight like unto an emerald. And round about the throne were four and twenty seats: and upon the seats I saw four and twenty elders sitting, clothed in white raiment; and they had on their heads crowns of gold... And in the midst of the throne, and round about the throne, were four beasts full of eyes before and behind. And the first beast was like a lion, and the second beast like a calf, and the third beast had a face as a man, and the fourth beast was like a flying eagle... And they were full of eyes within: and they rest not day and night, saying, Holy, holy, holy, Lord God Almighty, which was, and is, and is to come." Inspired by this resplendent vision, ablaze with jewels, many artists conjured up an image of it in the dimly lit crypts where the choir of monks could gaze at it when they assembled for their chants; then at the entrances of abbey churches, where it could catch the rays of the setting sun.

BOOK OF PERICOPES OF ABBESS UTA OF NIEDERMÜNSTER (1002-1025): THE CRUCIFIXION.
REGENSBURG, FIRST QUARTER OF THE 11TH CENTURY. FOLIO 3 VERSO, COD. LAT. 13 601, STAATSBIBLIOTHEK, MUNICH.

GOSPEL BOOK OF BISHOP BERNWARD OF HILDESHEIM: THE INCARNATION. ABOUT 1015.
FOLIO 174 RECTO, COD. 18, CATHEDRAL TREASURE, HILDESHEIM.

187

THE LAST JUDGMENT. TYMPANUM OF THE PORTAL OF THE ABBEY CHURCH OF BEAULIEU-SUR-DORDOGNE
(BEGUN BEFORE THE MIDDLE OF THE 12TH CENTURY).

THE MONOGRAM OF CHRIST FLANKED BY LIONS. LATE 11TH TO MID-12TH CENTURY.
TYMPANUM OF THE WEST PORTAL, CATHEDRAL OF JACA (HUESCA), SPAIN.

APSE MOSAIC IN THE LOWER CHURCH OF SAN CLEMENTE, ROME
(REBUILT IN 1108 BY POPE PASCHAL II).

SACRAMENTARY FROM THE CATHEDRAL OF SAINT-ETIENNE, LIMOGES: THE ASCENSION.
ABOUT 1100. FOLIO 84 VERSO, MS LAT. 9438, BIBLIOTHÈQUE NATIONALE, PARIS.

CROSS OF QUEEN GISELA OF HUNGARY. REGENSBURG, ABOUT 1006.
SCHATZKAMMER DER RESIDENZ, MUNICH.

In the portal of the oratory reserved for celebrations of the praise of God, the skies roll open; for it was here that illustrations of the text of the Apocalypse, initiations into the mystery of the Hereafter, were placed. At Saint-Benoît-sur-Loire they adorn the capitals of the gate-tower. At Saint-Savin painters represented Christ within the globe, His arms outspread, in the vestibule of the church. Two angels beside Him hold up the instruments of the Passion and he is attended by the strange beings peopling the vision of St John the Divine. No place could be better fitted for unveiling the mysteries of the invisible to the man who, turning away from the world, came to the church door so as to draw near to God; and for making known to him the divine event prefigured by the church in its entirety—the return of Jesus in power and glory—before he made his way into the flooding light of the chevet. The porch, a perfect cube, had the same dimensions as the holy Jerusalem seen by the Apocalyptist, "foursquare, and the length is as large as the breadth... Having the glory of God... her light was like unto a stone most precious, even like a jasper stone, clear as crystal." It had a wall great and high pierced with wide gates "and the foundations of the wall were garnished with all manner of precious stones... and the twelve gates were twelve pearls."

But before the light of the Lamb rose on the world, the four angels "holding the four winds of the earth" would raise their trumpets to their lips and sound the end of all things. Therefore it behooved him who entered the church to begin by destroying the seeds of corruption in his soul, stripping himself of his wealth, his weapons, his family, even his personal volition, as did the monk when he made his profession. Then and then only he could join the great procession faring to Jerusalem. "The nations of them which are saved shall walk in the light of it [the City] :and the kings of the earth do bring their glory and honour into it. And the gates of it shall not be shut at all by day: for there shall be no night there. And they shall bring the glory and honour of the nations into it. And there shall in no wise enter into it any thing that defileth, neither whatsoever worketh abomination, or maketh a lie: but they which are written in the Lamb's book of life." Romanesque art was the creation of a group of men who, fired with the love of God, sought to transcend in the cloisters the sordid mediocrity of the world around them, and, fascinated by these visions of the heavenly Jerusalem, set their course to the celestial heights. There at last, in those imagined splendors, their yearning for perfection would be satisfied. To make its earthly simulacrum they assembled all the treasures not to be found in their native land: gold, lapis lazuli, strange perfumes brought from the East. The monks by their daylong liturgy, the groups of pilgrims braving the perils on the way and, soon, the bands of crusaders—all alike advanced, side by side, towards this visionary goal.

BEATUS OF LIEBANA, COMMENTARIES ON THE APOCALYPSE: THE COMING OF THE END OF THE WORLD.
SAINT-SEVER, GASCONY, MID-IITH CENTURY. FOLIO 141 RECTO, MS LAT. 8878, BIBLIOTHÈQUE NATIONALE, PARIS.

BEATUS OF LIEBANA, COMMENTARIES ON THE APOCALYPSE: HORSEMEN OF THE APOCALYPSE. 1086.
FOLIO 151 RECTO, COD. 1, CATHEDRAL OF BURGO DE OSMA (SORIA), SPAIN.

FULDA LECTIONARY: THE ADORATION OF THE LAMB. LAST THIRD OF THE 10TH CENTURY.
FOLIO I VERSO, MS 2, HOFBIBLIOTHEK, ASCHAFFENBURG.

SACRAMENTARY FROM ST GEREON, COLOGNE: CHRIST ENTHRONED. 980-990.
FOLIO 15 VERSO, MS LAT. 817, BIBLIOTHÈQUE NATIONALE, PARIS.

CHRIST PANTOCRATOR. 1123. FRESCO FROM THE CHURCH OF SAN CLEMENTE, TAHULL.
MUSEO DE ARTE CATALAN, BARCELONA.

CHRIST. ABOUT 1000-1020. CENTRAL PART OF THE GOLD ALTAR IN AACHEN CATHEDRAL.

THE THRESHOLD

Christ Himself had said "I am the door," meaning a portal opening on the celestial world beyond our ken. Throughout the eleventh century an idea gained ground, *sub rosa* to begin with, that the terrible God of the Moissac porch, presiding a tribunal of judges, the God who showed His wrath by visiting mankind with pestilences, famines, wars and the cruel hordes of invaders who had but recently swept in from the East, leaving devastation in their wake—this God was after all not different from the Son; in other words, from man. Hence a tendency to stress the doctrine of the Incarnation, a tendency that was perhaps more active among the populace than in the cloisters.

This much is certain: that a spirit of unrest developed among the masses, setting them against the Church and moving them to lend a readier ear to the discourses of itinerant preachers, laymen and the hermits who, always abundant in Italy, had now taken to roving the countryside of France. These illuminati spoke of a poor God who took no pleasure in the gold heaped round Him by the priests; an inflexible God who disdained the prayers of a worldly, pleasure-loving clergy. For the rank and file of Christians the sacramental rites opened the door of salvation, and the reform movement in progress in the Church quickened their desire to see these propitiatory gestures made by purer hands.

This was what the townsfolk of Milan had in mind when they demanded that their priests abstain from women and revolted against their simoniac archbishop. They were infuriated by the moral decadence of the priesthood, whose task it was to ensure a "magical" communication between man and the divine. But what, one wonders, can it have been that incited the peasant from the Champagne region whom Rudolph Glaber describes as a madman to an iconoclastic frenzy, to tear down crucifixes and smash images of the Saviour? What attribute of divinity was specially revered by those thirteen

canons at Orléans "who seemed purer than the others" and whom King Robert in 1023 condemned to be burnt as heretics? And when the group in Aquitaine who "denied the virtue of the Cross, the efficacy of Holy Baptism, all the doctrines of the Holy Church, abstained from certain kinds of food, had the air of monks and feigned chastity," were suspected of leanings towards Manichaeism, was it not because they over-emphasized the conflict all men sensed between the God of the Bible and the powers of darkness and, in anguished expectation of the End of Time, rejected over-drastically all things carnal? Maybe they were also protesting against an excess of ritualism, and, tormented by the problem of the existence of evil in the world, perplexed by the mystery of the Incarnation, asked to be given more than mere ceremonial—a clearer explanation of the true nature of Christ and how it was that this divine essence should have dwelt among men and "saved their souls alive."

It was certainly the spiritual malaise of the age, this dissatisfaction with the *status quo*, now manifesting itself with ever-increasing intensity, that gave rise to the two movements which developed after 1050, within the Church itself. One was a tendency to discuss, using the apparatus of reasoning and dialectic, those central mysteries which were giving pause to the "plain man's faith": the Trinity, the Eucharist and indeed the whole question of the intervention of God in the affairs of men. Already in the reformed monasteries of Normandy John, a nephew of William of Volpiano, who in 1028 became abbot of Fécamp, had scrutinized the text of the Synoptic Gospels, seeking to discover means of delivering man from his condition, from the world of sin which held him in thrall. He saw in Jesus the Way, leading us to the light of Godhead. "He was circumcised so as to cut us free from the vices of the flesh and the mind; presented in the temple so as to bring us, pure and sanctified, towards God; baptized so as to wash us clean of our offences; tempted, so as to defend us against the onslaughts of the devil; made captive to free us from the power of the Enemy; mocked so as to rescue us from the derision of the demons; crowned with thorns so as to extricate us from the thorns of the primordial curse; raised on the cross to draw us to Him; given to drink of vinegar and gall so as to lead us to a land of endless joy; sacrificed, a lamb without blemish, on the altar of the cross so as to take away the sins of the world." John of Fécamp's theology followed the winding roads of the anagogical method; images and words join forces, all being oriented towards a theophany, a manifestation of the blinding light of God. It told of a mysterious alchemy whereby base matter is transmuted into the pure gold of the unknowable. But it also pointed the way to St Anselm's major work *Cur Deus homo?* Italian by birth, Anselm too was abbot of a Norman monastery; then, from 1094 to 1098 Archbishop of Canterbury. In *Cur Deus homo?* he answered the question asked in this title on scholastic lines and thus inaugurated the doctrine of the Incarnation which was to be bodied forth on so many Gothic monuments.

Meanwhile, finding the Apocalypse less inspiring than the rest of the New Testament, some monks began preaching against the ceremonial pomp and splendor of the Cluniac liturgy, and advocated a way of life that did not seek to imitate the glory of the seraphim, the grandeur of the New Jerusalem, but following in the footsteps of the Master, converted God's servants into true apostles, poor and humble. In 1088, the very year when Abbot Hugh installed the workyard of the new basilica, the great days of Cluny were over. A new type of monachism, all for austerity, was setting in. Priests were now disposed to lead a communal life like that of the monks, but without ceasing to go forth and preach the Gospel to the people, the body of canons was amending its ways, conforming to a stricter Rule, and, thanks to the activities of the Gregorian reformers, there was a revival of the dignity of the episcopate.

Thus the soil was prepared for the flowering of great cathedrals in the near future and, as the result of an intensification of the religious sensibility, less importance was attached to the ceremonial of the liturgy. What all thoughtful Christians wanted was a religion that no longer focused attention on the promised glories of the celestial Jerusalem but stressed the humanity of the Son of God.

This change in the spirit of the age was also promoted by the religious movements that led to the crusades. When, instead of descending into dark crypts to venerate relics of tutelary saints whose talismanic power had replaced that of the heathen gods, pilgrims elected to travel to the tomb of Christ, and when the penitential rites imposed on knights anxious for their soul's salvation diverted the aggressive instincts of these warriors towards a pious journey to the Holy Sepulchre, the Cross began to have a new significance. Hitherto it had been but one of many symbols of God's power over the universe. A cosmic sign conjoining Space and Time, a Tree of Life, it stood for the entirety of the cosmos, and if God had chosen it to be the instrument of his Son's death, this was by reason of its esoteric values. When Christ's body hung on it, He was not shown racked by pain, but as a crowned king, living and triumphant. The cross was in fact an emblem of victory and kings made much of it; King Robert even played the part of Jesus in the passion play of Holy Week. But gradually, after the year 1000, the symbol was given more actuality and, in the process, a new orientation. Thus when in 1010 a monk of the Abbey of Saint-Martial at Limoges saw "an enormous cross hovering in the sky with Our Lord's body hanging on it and an abundant rain of tears streaming from His eyes," this vision brought to his mind the sufferings of Christ. It was a similar emotional response that led the knights to observe the Truce of God every Thursday and Friday "in memory of the Last Supper and of the Passion of Our Lord." The ordering of golden crosses from the artificers working for the royal household and their distribution to churches had long been a privilege reserved to emperors and kings. Now, however, they lost this monopoly—as they were losing all their regal powers, which were passing into the hands of the feudal nobility. In the eleventh century more and more people wore crosses. In 1095 all who embarked on a journey to the Holy Land had the sacred sign sewn on their garments. Thus they too became avatars of Christ, as hitherto only anointed kings had been. It was the earthly life of God incarnate they were going to relive in Palestine. When in the year 1000 some learned clerics were asked "what such a great concourse of people at Jerusalem could signify," they replied that in their opinion it was a portent of "the coming of that son of perdition, Antichrist" and the imminence of the Last Day. Had it not been foretold that one premonitory sign would be that all the nations "made smooth the road of the East," by which he (the Antichrist) was to come and the nations prepare to go forth to meet him? But the pilgrims came back full of pregnant memories. Was it because he had visited the Holy Sepulchre so recently that the Count of Angoulême hoped to die "adoring and kissing the wood of our Saviour's cross"? This much is certain: that the many devout travelers who were to be seen in those days hastening like swarms of bees or migratory birds towards the Promised Land, prompted in many cases by the eschatological apprehensions of the age and fascinated by the prospect of setting eyes on the Holy City, returned to their villages, castles, cathedrals (if they had not died en route) with a new awareness of the living Jesus.

Did they already identify the Son of Man at whose tomb they had worshipped with the transcendent image of justice and domination that sculptors of the year 1100 were placing on portals of the abbey churches in which the "new" art was coming to fruition? In Carolingian times an important liturgical function was assigned to the church porch, for it was there that certain funerary rites were solemnized. Hence the emphasis on Christ the Saviour, and the placing in the porch of scenes of the Second Coming and the Last Judgment, pivot of the entire iconography of the age. The porch represented the celestial Jerusalem but also a way of access to the world of light awaiting the Christian on the day of resurrection. Suger was the creator, about 1140, of what we call the Gothic. But he was a member of the Benedictine Order and his theology, like that of all eleventh-century monks, was based on an elaborate system of analogies whose sequences and associations were thought to lead the questing spirit of the recluse to an understanding of the mysteries of godhead. He therefore adopted *in toto* the symbolism of Romanesque art, which may be said to culminate in his great Abbey of Saint-Denis. For its portal he composed dedicatory verses (which can be interpreted in various ways) setting forth the purport of the "noble work" he had in mind. "Of that which shines herein"—that is to say, within the edifice but also in the heart of the world, the heart of Time, the heart of man, the heart of God—"this golden door gives an intimation." Art, in other words, prefigures the transcendent realities which will be revealed to the human soul once it has crossed the barrier of death and seen the heavens opening to reveal the *verum lumen* (the True Light) on the Last Day. "For by way of material beauties the mind is elevated to true Beauty and by the light of its splendors raised up from the earth in which it lay buried, and enters into heaven." It is no overstatement to say of eleventh-century art that it makes God a visible presence, that it illuminates and aspires to proffer man the noblest means to rebirth in the world of light beyond the grave.

Among the many discoveries, inventions and changes in the field of creative art to which the making of the Christian West gave rise, none was more remarkable and unexpected than the deliberate return to monumental sculpture. Imbued with memories of classical antiquity, imperial art had for several centuries exalted the values of the free-standing figure realized in three dimensions of space, which gradually superseded the incised design and the tendencies to geometric abstraction and plant forms of barbarian art. The first bold forward step was taken by prelates of the Ottonian renaissance when they commissioned sculptures of sacred figures: Christ crucified and bronze reliefs of Biblical scenes. But the truly revolutionary move was made towards 1100 when in the Romanesque part of Christendom, in the provinces where Latinity had never wholly died out, sculptors were called on to make divine figures having the full plasticity of Roman statues. Benedictine monks had no qualms about placing them in the portals of the churches, no longer near the altar where they were almost hidden from sight during the services, but publicly, where all could gaze on them at leisure.

We have no means of ascertaining in what monastery this new departure, this triumph over the Christians' age-old mistrust of the evil lures of pagan statuary, originated. Which is the oldest Romanesque tympanum, that of Moissac or that of Cluny, is an open question. For the chronology of works of art in this period is highly conjectural. These carved figures were solemn offerings to Almighty God; they belonged to Eternity, not to Time, and no one thought of dating them. True, we have good reasons for believing that when St Hugh of Cluny undertook to embellish the edifice whose building he had undertaken, and whose every element he wished to decorate as soon as it was set in place, he summoned to the mother abbey the most skilled artisans in Christendom. Can it be assumed that the best of these sculptors had already carved the stone portals of the small churches in the Brionnais region whose adornments may be equally well regarded as belated reflections of the great Cluniac art? It seems safer to assume that the artists called on to devise the grandiose ensemble that about 1115 came into being at Cluny on the threshold of the largest basilica in the world —and, before this, to carve the capitals in the choir—took inspiration from models found in the ornamental work produced by the Mosan metalworkers, in which the classical traditions of Ottonian art continued to have an active part.

CHURCH OF SAINT-PIERRE AT MOISSAC, NEAR TOULOUSE: SOUTH PORTAL. 1110-1115.

CHURCH OF THE MADELEINE AT VÉZELAY, BURGUNDY: PORTAL OF THE NAVE. ABOUT 1120-1150.

CATHEDRAL OF SAINT-LAZARE AT AUTUN, BURGUNDY: MAIN PORTAL. ABOUT 1120-1130.

There can be no question that both Gislebertus, who signed his work at Autun, and the Vézelay master derived their skill perhaps, in any case their inspiration, from the famous workyard of Cluny. From the viewpoint of an historian of the culture and aesthetic sensibility of the age, all the large-scale works of this order, contemporary with the First Crusade and the wave of religious fervor that ensued, marked an important stage in the evolution of western Christendom. Hitherto images of Christ had never been located in the visible world. Even when they were not purely abstract, esoteric symbols in the form of the Cross, Alpha and Omega, or the sacred monogram were always given (as on the illuminated pages of Ottonian liturgic manuscripts) a completely unrealistic setting. The figures, too, without weight or thickness, remind us of Rudolph Glaber's description of the souls in Purgatory. All, in fact, belonged to that unseen realm whose underlying order was embodied in the architecture of the Romanesque church.

Thus at the very time when dialecticians in the chapter schools of Neustria were beginning to discuss the nature of the three Persons of the Trinity and trying to discover how God made Himself man, monumental sculptors were transposing these images from the supernatural world, bringing them down to earth and embodying them in the hardest, most durable material. In so doing they anticipated that trend of religious thought which was soon to replace the fantasies of the Apocalypse with the human virtues of the New Testament in the cathedrals of the Ile-de-France, virtues of which these images were incarnations.

True, one feels that the sculptor of the Moissac Christ, a despotic figure surrounded by the tetramorph and twenty-four music-making elders, was still poles apart from this humanized conception of Our Lord. But already in the Autun porch this distance is reduced; we see Jesus seated among the apostles, terrestrial beings, whose faces express love rather than numinous awe. We see these same apostles caught in the graceful swirling movement of the Vézelay tympanum, which evokes not the world invisible, but, for the first time, the world of man, the world whose time is measured by the twelve months of the year, and whose space extends to the confines of the world, peopled by strange races. It is as if, on the brink of the twelfth century, the Romanesque dream-world was fading out and the Gospel message at long last being diffused everywhere, freeing man from his atavistic fears and urging him on to conquest. On the threshold of Vézelay, where St Bernard was soon to preach a crusade before the King of France, there then arose the most majestic figure of the living God that Christendom had seen.

CHURCH OF THE MADELEINE AT VÉZELAY, BURGUNDY: CHRIST, DETAIL OF THE PORTAL OF THE NAVE. ABOUT 1120-1150.

INDEX OF NAMES

LIST OF ILLUSTRATIONS

PRINTED ON THE PRESSES OF
EDITIONS D'ART ALBERT SKIRA
15 FEBRUARY 1967

PHOTOGRAPHS BY

Alinari-Anderson, Florence (pages 44 top, 126), A.C.L., Brussels (pages 105 bottom, 106 top), Archives photographiques, Paris (pages 147, 148), Maurice Babey, Basel (pages 20/21, 36, 37, 44 bottom, 66/67, 69, 76 left and right, top and middle, 77 upper right and bottom, 78, 88, 96, 99, 101, 102, 107 lower left, 108, 117 top and bottom, 119, 121, 127 upper right and bottom, 128, 140, 141, 143, 149, 150, 161, 162/163, 164, 165, 166, 173 bottom, 175, 176 upper left, 188 top and bottom, 194, 197, 203, 204, 205, 207,) B. Henry Beville, Alexandria, Va. (pages 34, 118), Bernard Biraben, Bordeaux, by courtesy of the Commissariat Général au Tourisme de France (page 127 upper left), Robert Braunmüller, Munich (page 191), Claudio Emmer, Milan (page 29), Foto Fuchs, Aschaffenburg (page 195), Marc Garanger, Paris (page 142), Photographie Giraudon, Paris (page 45 left and upper right, 76 lower right), Atelier Niko Haas, Trier (page 106 bottom), A. F. Kersting, London (page 89), Raymond Laniepce, Paris (pages 24, 30, 87 top and bottom), Louis Loose, Brussels (pages 22, 39), Erwin Meyer, Vienna (page 14), Umberto Orlandini, Modena (page 65), Karl H. Paulmann, Berlin (page 176 lower right), Studio R. Remy, Dijon (pages 77, 105 top), Herbert Rost, Darmstadt (page 71), Jean Roubier, Paris (pages 43, 45 lower right, 46), Guido Sansoni, Florence (page 40), Oscar Savio, Rome (pages 139, 189), Scala, Florence (pages 138, 168), Schmölz-Huth, Cologne (pages 23, 198), Studio für Fotografie, Tübingen (page 120), Hermann Wehmeyer, Hildesheim (pages 35, 187), Yan, Toulouse (pages 100, 174 top and bottom), and the photographic services of the following libraries and museums: Bergen, Universitetet, Historisk Museum (page 75), Cologne, Kölnisches Stadtmuseum, Rheinisches Bildarchiv (page 107 upper right), London, British Museum (pages 26, 68), Munich, Bayerische Staatsbibliothek (pages 28, 33, 38, 169, 173 top, 186), Paris, Bibliothèque Nationale (pages 70, 90, 125, 170, 190, 193, 196). Photographic material for the illustration on page 27 kindly lent by Verlag Fredebeul & Koenen KG, Essen.

COLOR PLATES ENGRAVED BY GUEZELLE & RENOUARD, PARIS

BLACK AND WHITE PLATES BY IMPRIMERIES RÉUNIES, LAUSANNE

PRINTED IN SWITZERLAND